FREE TO LOVE

The Power of Being Moved with Compassion

a memoir

Lluvia DíazLanier

November Skies Publishing
PO Box 1563
Battle Ground, WA 98604

November Skies Publishing
PO Box 1563
Battle Ground, WA 98604

Free to Love is a memoir. It is a product of the author's recollection of events and timeline. The names and identifying details of some characters in this book have been changed or omitted.

First November Skies Publishing paperback edition 2023

Unless otherwise noted, all Scripture quotations are from the New King James Version of the Bible.

Cover design by Lluvia DíazLanier
Illustration by Sa Petite Fleur
Cover photograph by Darryl DíazLanier

Published by November Skies Publishing, a division of Legacy Media Group, Washington

6 5 4 3 2 1

Printed in the United States of America

ISBN: 979-8-9892728-0-8 (pbk)
ISBN: 979-8-9892728-2-2 (ebook)

To my children, their children, and all the generations to come

CONTENTS

PREFACE

My sweet reader, I am sharing my story to show the raw realities of life that hardships can bring. I have heard many heart aching stories from others who have experienced greater adversity. If you are one of those beautiful souls, I encourage you–Your story is not over.

This book is also for anyone coming alongside those facing unplanned pregnancies. You may be a parent, lover, sibling, friend, teacher, neighbor, etc., who could benefit from this book as it will give you insight to the roller coaster of emotions that come with making a decision.

I wrote my story in third person, not because I thought it would create a better story, because in actuality I believed it to be quite the opposite. I wrote it in third person by the inspiration of an early morning wake up call.

I woke up around 3AM on March 1, 2023 with beautiful eloquent sentences forming in my head. This has happened before and I have at times dismissed them and gone back to sleep thinking I will remember them, but in fact, I don't. This time, I began to write them down.

I knew I was to write this book about my life, but I questioned why these sentences were all in third person. To my surprise, embracing my memories and writing this through the possible perspectives of others brought me to tears. Those tears continued to flow for the duration of my writing. It brought forth beautiful and unexpected healing. A new level of compassion was able to form as I wrote what those in my story could have possibly experienced from the impact of my behavior.

While misunderstanding the purpose for this book, I could have easily dismissed the third person sentences but I am so thankful that I didn't. Had I done what others have done and written it in first person, I would have missed out on the opportunities to see life through the perspective of others.

During the writing process, I was prompted to find old writings I had written many years ago. Shockingly, I realized I had kept college papers, journal entries and poems dating back as early as 2000. As I continued to read the unexpected reminders of what I experienced, I knew these pieces must be included in the book. I included them not because I want to expose my dirty laundry, nor have pent up emotions I need to release, but to simply be real and transparent to the realities I faced. In doing so, I hope others who relate to any aspect of my journey would find hope to know there is more to life than the here and now.

These journal entries, poems, and letters captured my raw emotions displayed from an adolescent mind. Some poems might seem wonky and a little off and that's okay. Some letters might be lengthy and I might sound like a whiny baby–and that's okay. Again, some of these writings were written by my seventeen year old self full of mixed and confusing emotions.

These writings do not capture my now best friend and husband in a great light. However, we have come to agree that exposing the ugly realities some relationships might endure is paramount in bringing freedom and healing to all those who may need it.

May it be that you are merely reading this book at the suggestion of someone and have no interest in my story. Regardless of what compelled you to pick this book up, I pray you will experience a new level of compassion for yourself and those around you. Compassion has the potential to interrupt you and position you toward experiencing beautiful freedom–if you allow it. I pray you will experience freedom through this book.

CHAPTER 1

PAIN & DARKNESS

Lost and confused as to how her life brought her to this very moment, Jeanette took a deep breath. She stared in the mirror in confusion as to who was staring right back at her. Perplexed by the events that transpired in her life, she took another deep breath.

The eyes staring back at her were haunting. As if pleading with her for help. She could almost hear the girl on the other side of the mirror screaming for help. Jeanette forced a smile to cover up those expressive eyes. She felt that smile fade. She couldn't hold the facade for more than a few seconds. Yet, determined to make today great, she continued to practice. She sighed as her smile faded yet again.

Distracted again by the eyes staring at her very soul, she began shaking her head as if to tell her she can't come out. The intensity of those eyes subsided and Jeanette's smile protruded. She took a step forward and knew the significance of that one step just taken. More steps would be required of her, but she was ready.

The sun rose early that morning just like every day before that. This day was different for Jeanette, though. This day held possibilities beyond expectation. So much can come forth from today. Walking out today would require courage. Jeanette was holding on to courage by her fingertips and feared that at any moment courage could slip away. Still, her fears were entangled with hope. The first day at a new school was provoking emotions with the potential to cripple her steps.

Intertwined feelings of nervousness and excitement filled Jeanette's body. She had been expecting this day since the transfer papers were submitted by her parents. Transferring schools seemed like the only solution at the time. Jeanette had been stuck in a dark place for a few years now. So dark and confusing that both her parents and principal thought best for her to start fresh at a new school.

"Start fresh?" What did that even mean to a girl who felt lonely, unheard and misunderstood? How does a new high school swarmed with unfamiliar people help a girl who was willing to take her own life? No one really knew the outcome to this decision but it just seemed right to remove her from her environment of comfort and place her in a new and unknown environment. Her parents nor existing school were at capacity to walk with her in this dark road, so plucking her out and sending her off to another school seemed best. "Maybe the change of scenery would help her snap out of it," was their reasoning.

So there she went, with an unspoken "tag you're it" to the new school. Maybe this new environment would be the place where she can "snap" out of it, she told herself. "How did I even snap into this, let alone snap out of it?" she wondered. This snapping into place makes more sense for something tangible like building blocks. Humans are much more complex than building blocks which fit perfectly into place. "How did I even get here?" she cried out in wonder as to how she arrived in this dark and lonely place.

Lost and confusion surrounded her with the question as to how her life brought her to this very moment. "Did one event have the power to deter me *this* greatly from what life used to be?" She pondered. Or was it a series of events that led her to make impulsive and self gratifying decisions without worry of consequences? Or was her brain just not fully developed to make each decision that would present itself before her? Regardless of how she got there, she knew she was there. "I'm here now, and need to figure out how to get out," she concluded.

All of this took place during a time when mental health awareness was in its developing stages. Doctors at the hospital Jeanette had recently stayed at medicated her believing to balance the chemicals in her brain back to "normal." She didn't feel any different, though. She felt just as inconvenient as she had before. She felt just as hungry for love but didn't know how to express it. She just couldn't seem to formulate thoughts to express this void inside her. She was on a path in search of filling that emptiness.

Jeanette stared at the note card of a puppy on the cover with her dad's writing inside. "I'm sorry," were the words enlarging from the paper. Sadness filled her heart and she felt the pain her dad expressed in those two words. "He tries really hard to love me," she thought. "Why isn't it enough?!" she screamed silently.

Her search and longing were paving a path for her. Before she realized it, she had become numb and was nonchalantly walking this path out. This frivolous and carefree walk led her down a place she never intended to go. She was now positioned as a prime target for promiscuity.

Her promiscuous behavior set her up in the trajectory of heartache. She didn't know her search for love and affirmation would cost so much. She was ignorant to the fact that the price she would pay for love was more than she had.

The rejection from the guys crushed her spirit. But it was the hurt she experienced from the cliques of girls that deepened those wounds within her heart. It's one thing to feel a cut from a blade, it's another thing to feel it with serrated edges. Those perfect Barbie dolls were the serrated edges.

Jeanette was a tough cookie though. She was not about to let people know they had the power to hurt her. Those deep wounds led to a build up around her heart, similar to scar tissue building up from a physical injury. Scar tissue grows through the healing process and can act as a self preservation mechanism protecting the body from further injury. Through the process of skin repairing itself, scar tissue works to close the gaps and repair the wound. This protects the body from further injury or infection.

The problem with developing hard-like scar tissue around her heart is that it doesn't stop trying to heal and protect her. Each circumstance has the potential for another layer of growth of protection. These layers created a wall which had been built to protect her hurting heart. Before Jeanette knew it, she found herself locked inside the very wall she created–a dark lonely place that was intended to protect her, not imprison her.

No one could hear Jeanette screaming silently to be freed from the terror filled days and nights that ate at her confidence. Relocating her prison was the best way to help this girl who was "screaming for attention". Yes, attention is what she was after. She yearned for love and acceptance, deeper than what she had imagined. Her family and friends tried but they couldn't break through this condensed heavy wall that barricaded her. Her heart of stone was not only blocking those trying to express love, but it felt as if it was closing in on her causing her to panic and wish for life to be over.

The memory of the ambulance taking her away was hazy yet vivid. She heard the paramedics asking her questions; her name, date of birth and possibly more. She felt sick to her stomach staring at the ceiling of that ambulance. "What did I do?" she questioned herself. "Why did I do this?" she continued. Lost in her misery, she hadn't seen another way out but to ingest a bottle filled with pills earlier that day.

It was a low risk way to end things just in case she changed her mind. And change her mind, she did! She called her best friend to thank her for her friendship; to say her "good-bye" without actually saying good-bye. This friend knew her well. She could distinguish the tone and pitch of her sorrow filled voice. Jeanette wouldn't tell her anything except sob in gratitude and sorrow. This concerned friend called the police. Unsure what the emergency was, the calvary of emergency responders were dispatched and she ran several blocks to Jeanette's house.

After taking care of the toxins Jeanette ingested, she was put on watch and transferred to College Hospital in Costa Mesa, California. There she received daily intensive treatment with behavioral interventions. They were on a mission to reinforce progress toward their established treatment goals. It was a scary place to be at.

The next wing down held wailings that gave Jeanette the chills. The adolescent patients with her in that hospital made up stories of the patients in those connecting wings. Thankful for the locked doors that separated the adults from her wing, she cried herself to sleep.

She shook her head to bring herself back to the comfort of her own room. Brushing her hair, she began to drift back into memories of sorrow, but quickly she tried to pull herself back into reality. She did not want to start today with those intrusive thoughts. They have a way of leading her with little control for her to hold on to happiness. As strong as she thought she was, she was no match for those destructive thoughts. She saw the height to the walls of her castle magnify to new heights. She felt so small compared to the massive wall.

This wall, as ugly as it was, was in fact her masterpiece. It was artwork from the depth of her being. This wall she had built was constructed from each moment of pain that had entered her life. Each moment someone teased her about her broken English; each moment someone commented on the color of her skin; each moment someone looked down on her body size; each moment someone overlooked her; each moment someone judged her.

Those moments added up throughout her days, turning into years resulting in an encircling wall where she stacked pain upon pain just as a mason stacks brick upon brick. Not only was pain in the equation, but similar to baking, her behavior acted like yeast to those painful moments causing each to expand. This well fed wall grew faster than she had ever intended.

It's a mystery as to why and how some can build platforms for their stage while others build walls from their very pain. Could it be similar to the characteristics of having food allergies or food intolerances? Several people can enjoy peanut butter and jelly sandwiches while others cannot. Their bodies react. Some people are just prone to food intolerances. Are some people just prone to pain intolerances? There happens to be an adverse reaction to their pain that leads them to build walls like built up tissue tries to protect its injury.

This mystery was not on Jeannette's mind though. Her mind was overtaken by fear. Deciding what to wear was not the problem of the day as most would think though. She'd been anticipating this day so her outfit was awaiting her. No, her physical appearance was on the back burner for the moment. Being lost was her greater fear. Not knowing the campus and looking like a fool was the real fear. The fear of embarrassment strangled her every breath. Some laugh off their embarrassment while others run away and hide. She was the type who hid.

Her third grade experience pierced her mind. She squirmed in her seat attempting to get her teacher's attention, but couldn't in time. She raced to the bathroom to relieve herself, but found herself surrounded with urine all over her pants. She stayed in that stall for what seemed like an eternity until someone finally noticed her absence and found her in her mess.

Those puffy eyes and tear-filled shirt were not met with compassion for her attempt but instead they were met with eyes of displeasure. Her eight year old limited mind interpreted them and perceived that she was an inconvenience to those that had to help. Unsure how her mom took time off work to race to her rescue, she embraced and accepted her mom's love. Her mom wiped every tear from her face that day. With her limited English vocabulary, Jeanette's mom advocated for her. Unsure how her mom did it, Jeanette was given an unlimited pass to use the restroom whenever she needed.

Jeanette's mom expressed her love in all the most beautiful ways she could with her broken English. And yet, moments, like her third grade incident, of being an inconvenience weighed heavily on her without even realizing it. These life moments added to the enclosure of her prison.

Fear of this unknown school campus was the very ingredient that was now forming a new stone to add to her collection. Her collection of stones were preparing for yet another layer to be built upon her wall. For the time being, it was just forming. No stone was fully created and a new layer was not yet added. Jeanette fought herself. She wrestled those fearful thoughts. Every ounce of her had to stay positive in order to survive.

The warmth of the early September air filled the sky as Jeanette braced herself to fight towards freedom. She pasted on a smile ready to conquer her day. She decided that since this is the fresh start everyone was raving about that she would change her name to make it official. Instead of going by her middle name, Jeanette, she would go by Lluvia, her first name.

Lluvia was the name she knew from early childhood until her parents decided to protect her from the teasing this name caused. Lluvia, pronounced "you-vee-ah", is the Spanish word for rain. Her cousins and friends decided to have fun with her name and thought it amusing to call her Storm or Thunder in Spanish. "Ay viene la Lluvia! Correle, la Tormenta te va llevar!" she heard faintly as if from a distance.

Nearing the school, she dismissed those voices. Lluvia's mom drove into the parking lot of this new school. Lluvia was dropped off like all others in the line of cars in front of her. She took a deep breath, stepped out of the car and walked nervously around the school in search of her classroom.

Walking into an almost full classroom, Lluvia scanned the room. She apprehensively took a seat by giggly girls who looked her up and down. After roll call and the teacher butchering her name, she found herself herded from her homeroom to the gym along with what appeared to be the whole student body.

With the speeding increase of her heart beat came more blood flow pumping through her body. She soon felt the nervous sensation of needing to relieve herself. "Oh no! What if I need to pee? Where's the bathroom?!" she nervously thought and immediately slowed her breathing. Thankfully, her bladder had been strengthened throughout the years since her 3rd grade experience.

The panic to find a bathroom subsided as she took slow breaths to calm herself down. She was shuffled into a row to find her seat on a bleacher next to what appeared to be uncaged animals. The gym was swarming with students yelling and calling for each other in hopes to find seats next to one another.

As she sat there observing the frenzy, she instantly sank in her loneliness. With her head on a swivel, she scoured, but didn't know one single person there. In her isolated pursuit to avoid being the only loner in the gym, she regained consciousness that she was sinking into self pity.

She soon snapped out of her daze of friendless pity. She was comforted by her protective mechanism. Hiding in plain sight was her super power. The tilt of her head brought both her hair and eyes toward the same direction. Downward, she gazed at her feet. She was in place to protect herself from any form of discomfort within the large fish tank-like gym had in store. It was one key element to ensure she wouldn't have any eye contact with those around her.

Similar to the deceptive game of peek-a-boo with a baby or toddler, Lluvia was sure that if she didn't make eye contact with others that her invisible powers were in effect. Her memories in middle school produced this proof that it worked. That day was no different. Not one person spoke to her. Not one person tried to get her attention. Not one person seemed to notice her. She was invisible to everyone around her. She made it out without a scratch of a glance. She was safe. Or so she thought.

Chapter 2

SCIENCE CLASS ATTRACTION

As Lluvia sat in her science class later that day, the most stunning young man she had ever laid her eyes on entered. His spiked bleached hair, enticing green eyes, body piercings, and plain white t-shirt captivated her attention. This gorgeous teenage boy could have decided to wear a closet full of options and yet a white t-shirt was his choice for the first day of school. That spoke volume to his level of confidence. He was so confident in himself that he did not need a loud shirt to draw attention to himself.

The way he walked, talked, and caused those around him to laugh and brighten up appealed considerably to Lluvia. She was mesmerized. Through her insecurities, she maintained her distance and observed this attractive guy from afar. She dismissed the absurd thought he could be attracted to her, she became okay with knowing he was unobtainable. Dreaming about him was the closest she could get at the moment. She was content with that.

The first week progressed like any other first week of school; full of introductions, syllabi, and awkward moments of attempts to navigate around the campus. After many corrections on the pronunciation of her name, Lluvia was beginning to question the ability to start fresh with a new name.

Lluvia is not an easy name to pronounce for English speakers. It was becoming more of a nuisance than she had anticipated. Disturbed by this new reality, Lluvia debated changing it back to Jeanette. She was not only the new girl who transferred half way through high school, but her difficult name soon exposed the weakness to her invisible power. Some people continued to call her Lluvia while others relievingly accepted Jeanette as her name.

The days of 11th grade homework increased as teachers began their lessons and the expectations of their students accelerated. Jeanette's bedroom became the home to the new textbooks that required reading night after night. Although her eyes were reading words in these books, her mind would wander to the gorgeous sixteen year old boy in her science class.

Daydreaming about his muscular arms holding her while he gazed into her eyes was luring her away from her studies. This ability to rest in his arms drew her to even more fantasies with this light-toned hunk.

Images of herself in scenes from movies with this handsome young man danced in her mind.

In class it was no different. She would find herself daydreaming about him. Her new friends exposed her secret to this boy early that September month. Embarrassment flushed her face in red complexion, but fled immediately after he asked her for her number.

Her mind couldn't figure out what he saw in her that caused him to talk to her. She was short for words. She fumbled through even the words she did have. Her insecurities alerted her with confusion as he put his arm around her shoulder while they walked down the stairs toward their next class. She was unsure of where this was headed, but she was ready for an adventure with this confident football player.

Darryl and Jeanette began to spend time together. Darryl introduced her to his friends and she did the same, but as time went by, they would find themselves eating lunch together away from any other friends. They found a nook by some stairs where they could fill their teenage hormones with steamy make-out sessions. This was a time before schools monitored their campuses with cameras. Their secret was hidden.

These kisses led to more physical touch. They began to explore each other's body and play a game called Nervous. This game consisted of touching each other's body and finding the spots that made each other nervous. As Jeanette touched Darryl's arms then his chest which led to his abs, he would become nervous as any other 16 year old would. His hormones were igniting.

This wasn't the first time she had caressed a male physique, but he didn't know that. He wasn't giving much thought as to how she knew how to excite him. He was just enjoying her provocative touch. They spent most of their lunch time alone without anyone to judge their behavior.

As the school year continued, they seemed to be inseparable. Every free moment was spent with each other. They paired up for a science research presentation on Mount Mauna Loa in Hawaii. This allowed for legitimate time together outside of school. The time outside of school did not stop there. In order to spend more time together, they decided to ditch school.

Ditching school meant she needed to have a reason prepared for her absence in case her parents ever asked. She needed a believable lie. She practiced and came up with lies, but were weak and she knew her parents would see right through them. Darryl taught Jeanette how to lie that day as they walked the long stretch of Chapman Blvd. in Fullerton, CA. Up until that point, Jeanette had never heard a lie sound so much like the truth before. Darryl didn't just fabricate a lie like she knew how. He embedded his lie with so much truth, it could not be recognized.

She was awed by his creativity. She couldn't believe he was her boyfriend! Not only was he gorgeous and he liked her and her curvy and non-petite body, but he was brilliant too! She recognized his talent of deception. She had never known anyone who could speak lies that were so convincing. You would think this to have been a red flag to Jeanette, but she was blinded by his charm. To her defense, no one knows they are being deceived as that's the beauty of deception. Little did she know that she would soon be the recipient of those lies.

Having Darryl brilliantly and creatively assemble her lies allowed for more opportunities to play their new loved game of Nervous, but on a more intimate level. Jeanette had only been dating Darryl for four months before giving herself away to him. Her sixteen year old mind could not have foreseen the emotional danger to follow.

Remember, Jeanette was a prime target for promiscuity and the byproducts that comes with it. Knowing she could not be that beautiful blonde who was perfect at everything, she had to offer something else to the boy who thought she was cute. She thought she only had a socially awkward, unconfident, self-conscious Jeanette to offer. Her massive desire to be part of a relationship where she was truly accepted and loved for who she was, were the only thoughts she entertained. This desire to be accepted and loved led her to make poor decisions; one after another.

Growing up all Jeanette wanted was to experience being loved. She desired being wanted, pursued and accepted. Her parents loved her the best way they knew how, but there was still a void in her adolescent heart. She turned her focus in pursuit to receive this love she'd been searching for. This led her down the dark path she didn't even know she had entered into.

Her adolescent years of walking in rebellion and drinking came shortly after entering the 9th grade. Somehow wearing make-up and being noticed by boys was more desirable than it had ever been. She would sneak around putting make-up on at school, and taking it off before she got home. She did not understand the reasoning behind my parents' strict rules. She wondered why she couldn't be like all the other normal girls and wear make-up and shave her legs! She desperately desired to find her sense of belonging. She dreamed of finding it with a guy who would love her.

During that first year of high school, her parents didn't sit her down to discuss things with her. They didn't walk her through their fears of her turning out to be like them. They just held what felt to Jeanette as a "tight leash". She wasn't allowed to hang out at the mall like her friends did. Her friends knew it was pointless to invite her; they knew Jeanette's dad would say "no."

Her dad thought it was frivolous to hang out at the mall. He worked in a store at a mall and saw more than his share of teenage ruckus. Little did he know how badly Jeanette desired to have a montage of trying on clothes with friends, taking pictures and feeling beautiful. She just wanted to feel beautiful. She just wanted to feel loved. She just wanted to feel wanted.

Jeanette found herself sneaking around behind her parents' back doing exactly what they feared she would do. Growing up in Southern California she was drawn to the fantasy the movie companies produce. She believed the illusion Hollywood portrayed about love. They made it appear so glamorous and she was entranced by it. The romantic comedies intrigued her, and she desperately wanted to feel loved like the characters in those movies.

All these thoughts motivated her behavior and she had her first kiss in 9th grade. It was the worst kiss she had ever had, but that one kiss led to the belief that the next guy would be better.

Due to the lack of confidence in who she was, she allowed the words boys spewed out of their mouths to entice her and in the end trap her. Jeanette's parents might have been a bit extreme to try to "protect" her from boys as if they were some sort of contagious disease. In their eyes, they might as well have been. This desire to be affirmed became such an addictive behavior for Jeanette. That is all she craved. It was as if she was magnetically drawn without much self control to refrain from it. She desperately desired it and her behavior showed it.

The things that once interested her, no longer did. She had lost herself. She didn't know who she was anymore. She no longer danced because she loved it and was passionate about it. No, she now danced to get attention, a comment, an affirmation, a pat on the back. She no longer did anything because she loved it, she was now after assurance that she was worth hanging out with.

The decision to start drinking alcohol at age 14 didn't come because she wanted to, but because her circle of influence encouraged and pressured this behavior. If only she knew the motives behind the encouragement to drink. She was so naïve in her way of thinking. Her parents were right to try to protect her from boys. Her parents weren't fools, they understood more than she gave them credit for.

Shortly after beginning her relationship with Darryl, she truly believed she had found the one. Jeanette was in love. And yet her longing for love caused her to make decisions that ended up with regrets. That January morning of 2000 she lost her virginity and became sexually active. Soon after that their relationship took on a different form. Little by little their relationship began to deteriorate. An alertness of dangers ahead began to ring loud. Self protection was armoring for what was ahead.

Darryl and Jeanette's only form of self preservation was morphed into playing mind games against each other. Although playing mind games was a new thing for them, it seemed to come naturally. Making each other jealous was what they thought they needed in order to feel validated.

Darryl and Jeanette played this mind game frequently.

"If he loves me," Jeanette thought, "he would not like it if another guy was finding me attractive and pursuing me." If he does not care what the other boys do, then she would think Darryl did not care about her. She used moments like this to define and measure his love for her. Darryl approached their relationship similarly. She was constantly testing him to see if his love for her was real.

These mind games evolved and withholding their thoughts and emotions from each other became their new way of feeling mature. They thought that bottling these feelings would show how mature they were and would prove to the other person that the things being done were not affecting them. But things did in fact affect them. These unhealthy mind games set them up for continual failure.

Darryl did not always respond with jealousy though; he bottled it all up and then responded with excessive anger for the smallest minute misunderstandings. Jeanette returned this anger with cutting words. They were at war and words were their strongest weapons. They fought constantly. They no longer knew how to express their feelings toward each other, because they were always trying to protect themselves *from* each other. Jeanette was prideful and did not want Darryl to know how his lies and deceptions affected her. She was doing the same bottling up of emotions as he was and did not even know it.

Jeanette feared that revealing her true heart

wrenching emotions of jealousy would make her vulnerable and weak. She worried that if he saw a glimpse of jealousy in her that he would leave her for being too clingy. Boys his age were always complaining about clingy girlfriends. So she shielded her pain and did her best not to make a big deal that he was hanging out with girls and lying to her about it. But it hurt Jeanette deeply. It crushed her. She didn't want to admit the depth of her pain, but instead hid away in her dark mansion she had created for herself. She refused to let him visit her there.

The fighting continued to damage their relationship. Things became worse once she was faced with a bigger fear than not finding the bathroom on the first day of school. Fear was just the tip of the iceberg though. Underneath was a far larger unseen monstrosity. As fear sank in, horror seeped in every crevice of her mansion as if to suffocate her with this dense fog.

Dread was settling in her prison which caused a paralytic level of distress in Jeanette's heart. Her feet felt weighted and locked into the ground beneath her. She couldn't breathe, let alone move. Panic filled her thoughts as if she were sinking deeper and deeper into this fear and drowning without the possibility of catching her breath.

Jeanette needed to come up for air if there was any way to survive this. Just one ounce of oxygen could move her powerless body. But she couldn't even gasp for air. It was as if she'd forgotten how to breathe. She felt herself fading in heavier darkness than before. Alarmed by this new level of darkness, she frantically wrestled her thoughts. Furiously she fought her way back.

She instantly remembered how to breathe! She caught her breath and sank back into the enclosed comfort of fear. It wrapped around her almost as if to comfort her that she was not alone. But she felt very much alone. She was alone facing the biggest fork in decision-making history. She was now face to face with a horrendous monster-like decision.

Every decision, good or bad, comes with a consequence. The decision she made 6 weeks prior to standing in that building was evident. Her parents' greatest fear for her life was no longer on the horizon. Instead, she was right in the thick of it. Had she not been chasing after love, she would definitely not have found herself in the situation she was facing.

Jeanette left the clinic that day confused, sorrowful and full of regrets. Tears ran down her face as she continued to think of her next move. She was at a stand-still, but she knew she could not stay there for too long. She needed to make a decision.

The weight of the mixed feelings made it difficult for a decision to surface to her mind. She had three choices in front of her. She knew what the right thing to do was, but to continue this path brought fears that she had never expected to face at that age. The three choices she had were not the three choices she wanted. Not deciding on any choice consequently was a decision as well. She was cornered and must choose one. Any one of these choices she made would change her life forever.

Jeanette changed her life forever. Hearing the words, "the test came back positive. You're pregnant" was ringing in her ears. To hide her sin and shame is the most logical thing to do. To expose her sexually active life to the world would bring judgment. She was already feeling like a failure at life. She is now sixteen and needing to face a giant life-changing decision that she was not prepared to make.

"To not abort means telling the world through a pregnancy-filled belly that they were right and that I would not amount to anything." She wrestled in her mind. The internal struggle of this decision brought intense turmoil. Thoughts invaded without any form of defense. She felt as if she really had the devil on her left shoulder and God on her right shoulder, like cartoons she had watched as a child, telling her all the reasons for each choice.

"No longer could I continue school," she thought. "My due date is a month before graduation," she continued. Experiencing this debate in her head felt like the literal back and forth pulling of tug-of-war. "Agh! This painful feeling in the pit of my stomach and throat closing in would be nothing compared to what my future holds," she imagined.

Jeanette desperately wanted to be a regular teenager and do regular teenager things. Being a regular teenager, now came with a price. It meant giving up part of herself; her child. Prior to this moment, Jeanette didn't believe in abortions, and yet all of a sudden that thought blasted in her mind as a blow horn demands attention.

Being a petrified sixteen year old, abortion now looked differently; as if it had taken on a different shape to her Catholic-upbringing memories. It seemed like such a simple and easy way of getting her life back and the way she wanted it. Deep down she knew that doing the fast and easy was not always the right thing to do and still, she couldn't see another way out.

"To go through with either of the three choices is permanent," she thought. "There is no going back on the decision made," she continued the wrestling match. Once the decision is made, it must be confirmed with her signature. To sign that form brought her to her knees in desperation to what this anguish filled fork meant. "That signature would only be the beginning," she stewed. "Then medication or worse, an invasive procedure!" she sweated. "Once that's completed it cannot be erased," fear gripped her. " It cannot be control+alt and deleted. It is permanent."

The decision to make life easier is always to abort the baby. Abortion wipes the reality of pregnancy's existence altogether. It enables the mother to continue with the existing lifestyle and not make any sacrifices to dreams, goals and ambitions. To entertain the thought of raising the child brought the most excruciating fears to Jeanette. Perplexed, she continued on this train of thoughts, "Even parents who plan pregnancies and are financially, emotionally and mentally prepared find themselves facing similar fears, what made me any different?"

Life as she knew it will forever change. Another human will need to be the center of her life. "Parents no longer have the freedom to do as they wish!" she sobbed. "Sacrifices will need to be made if the decision to have a full term pregnancy is followed with parenting." she cried in restlessness.

"I'm 16!" she cried out. A new thought popped in her mind that shook her to her core. "If I keep this baby, I have to tell my parents!" She sobbed immensely.

Teenage pregnancies hold more challenges than just the decision making process of the three options. They face the possibility of being out in the world alone and without support. "Worse, they can face forced abortions, forced marriages or forced to put the baby up for adoption through manipulation or coercion," Jeanette's mind rambled through these fears. Her mental state was now on high speed into understanding the realities of teenage pregnancies. She did not feel hopeful and being forced to do anything was not something she was willing to embrace.

A few days later, she opened up the phone book to the A's section to find an abortion clinic. She stared at the yellow pages of that book as she heard the voice on the other line. The Yellow Pages is a grand book of companies that offer every type of service in the county one resides in. This alphabetically organized list of organizations was her start. She entertained the thought of abortion several times and finally stood face to face with that path.

With the phone to her ear, she took a deep breath. For days Jeanette had been wrestling with the decision to abort or to follow through with the pregnancy. "Was the way "out" the way to go?" she thought to herself. "Is this my only feasible option?" "Why do I need a way "out" in the first place?" "Or can I find a way through it?" was her next thought. She ended the call without scheduling an appointment.

It turned out the ads in these yellow pages were creatively marketed. Under the A's for abortion, she called the clinic that said, "Looking for an abortion?" It in fact was a life affirming clinic; the sister clinic to the clinic that broke the news of her pregnancy.

The soft spoken and gentle voice on the other line encouraged her to come in so they could discuss options. She thanked her but rejected the invitation to entertain anything but an abortion. She then saw another ad on the following page and called that number. In her delirious state, she didn't realize she had dialed the same number as before.

The same soft spoken and gentle voice responded with, "honey, I just spoke to you, like I said, we don't offer abortions at this clinic. But we would love the opportunity to talk with you about other options and how we can be here along the way in whatever you decide." Embarrassment and frustration flooded Jeanette's face. She apologized, thanked the lady quickly, and declined her invitation.

Jeanette's Catholic upbringing could have been the underlying factor that established her foundation and her inner moral compass. From an outsider's perspective of her promiscuous behavior, it could appear that her moral compass was broken. The fruit of that was made known throughout all those moments of poor decision-making that led to this very fork she faced. But something inside her knew she couldn't have an abortion. It was an uneasy feeling that would nudge her and require her attention as a light does within peripheral vision.

Unsure of what it was that caused her to change her mind, she accepted the invitation to hear of her options and received a free ultrasound. Jeanette went back to Livingwell Pregnancy Center, the crisis pregnancy center that broke the news of her pregnancy. Their "mission is to provide alternative services and practical solutions to each woman facing an unplanned pregnancy, in order to allow her to make a rational decision without the undue pressure of her other circumstances." They emphasize on helping women with her unique situation, as well as preserving the life of the unborn child. They want the women who enter their doors "to know that they are loved and cared for by their staff and by God"

(Livingwell Pregnancy Centers, 2019).

Staring at the now closed book of yellow pages, her mind took her to a memory. At Livingwell, the lady at the center who had originally broken the news of the positive test result had prayed with Jeanette. Although Jeanette didn't quite understand the prayer, she felt cared for and saw a glimpse of hope through the love from the staff there. Unknowing of her pregnancy, she expected to feel judged and yet that feeling of being judged was completely absent. She did not expect to feel this love. She expected shame and guilt. She expected God to be mad at her. This love without shame and judgment from this stranger felt foreign to her and yet warmed her heart. Up until that point she had never experienced love that didn't come attached with anything else.

Their sincere love and understanding of her situation might have been what drew her back to their resources and the acceptance of the free ultrasound. Confusion as to why she was even entertaining this thought lingered in her mind as she redirected her steps from preferring an abortion to accepting this love. A newfound feeling of hope began to grow within Jeanette.

At the ultrasound appointment Darryl and Jeanette walked hand in hand. Nervously awaiting the ultrasound technician to see them they just stared at each other in silence and fear. With deep eyes of sorrow and joy Darryl pulled Jeanette closer to him in hopes to reassure her that they were in this together.

Both of their hearts raced as they walked this undetermined terrain of potential parenthood. Darryl was unaware of Jeanette's battle that led to being in that waiting room. He was unaware of her phone calls to end the pregnancy.

They held hands as they heard their baby's heartbeat for the first time. The patterned swooshing sound coming forth from that machine activated a gentle stream of tears to run down Jeanette's face. The fear that gripped Jeanette's heart that day as she stared at the ultrasound picture is one of the most pivotal moments she had faced thus far in her life. That day, she knew there was no turning back. She was about to engage in a life full of risks and challenges. She knew she was about to embark on more than just an adventure, but a roller coaster full of ups and downs.

Jeanette's perception of God was formed by her family's occasional visits to mass, church service. But within her limited knowledge of God, she knew she couldn't murder this baby, no matter how small. She heard its heartbeat. "It's alive!" She internally yelled. "I'm keeping you," she told her baby. That moment, she understood that her moral compass was not as broken as she had thought it was.

There were more tear-filled moments than she knew her body could produce. These tears were not all from fears & sorrows, but sprinkled in there were glimpses of hope. She was learning that this was a new chapter of her life and it can be anything she wanted it to be. She can either let it ruin her life, or she can make it work towards a better life. But as reality hit and she stared at that ultrasound picture, her heart immediately sank at the thought of telling her parents. She once again felt like her life was over.

Chapter 3

THE ROLLER COASTER OF JOY AND FEARS

Summer of 2000, leading into Senior year, was full of anguish and torment; not nearly the dream Jeanette had once anticipated. As she stared at the white playful geese on the man-made lake in Anaheim, California, she knew she needed to reveal the pregnancy to her parents. She had called in from work and taken that day off to mentally and emotionally prepare.

Formulating and structuring the sentences correctly to deliver a well thought of speech, seemed hopeless. Jeanette's emotions were still too raw to articulate the truth of her soon growing body. She sat there gazing and soaking in the beautiful summer weather. Maybe it was the vitamin D she was receiving from the sun or the joy in hearing the birds singing, or calmness of the water that induced her with bravery. Whatever it was didn't matter at the time, what mattered was that she felt ready for any backlash she would receive.

As she stepped foot into her house and heard her mom's judgemental questioning voice asking her why she wasn't at work, it was as if all her mental preparation vanished and disappeared from her mind. She spewed out in her normal self-defending voice that she was pregnant. There it was. She just announced it, without any form of consideration to how her mom would feel in receiving that blow to the stomach.

She had grown accustomed to her yelling matches with her mom. It always ended the same with Jeanette not allowing sadness to live in her mansion. She would instantly convert sadness into anger. This ensured sadness would suffocate and not live within her. Yelling matches were easier when she realized she had the power to refashion sadness into anger. Anger could speak in whatever manner necessary for self protection. Anger could care less about hurting others as long as it was doing its job and protecting Jeanette from feeling pain and sadness. Anger had brilliant tactics. It knew how to deny entry rights to pain and sadness. They were prohibited from occupying Jeanette's heart. Sadness was not her friend and she would avoid it at all costs.

Jeanette's mom, Esmeralda, was in shock. Jeanette

thought she almost saw her lose her balance. A whirlwind of emotions ran through Esmeralda's body. Esmeralda knew the realities Jeanette's future held. She herself was pregnant with Jeanette at sixteen. She rationalized that moment within herself that she was at least married.

Esmeralda's life was not all that much easier though. She dropped out of high school to take care of Jeanette. "Jeanette isn't even married!" she screamed internally. "Who's going to help her with a baby?" she continued. "What will she do with a baby?" she argued in her mind. As thoughts continued to race in this mental battle, she suddenly felt churning within her stomach. She was either going to vomit or pass out, or worse; both.

She was so consumed by her gripping thoughts, she left Jeanette and Darryl and retreated to her room. She would have to face this later. Later she would not be alone. Later, she could face it alongside her husband, Eddie, Jeanette's dad. In this overpowering loss of control, she didn't have the strength for yet another verbal wrestling match with Jeanette. She needed her husband's support to face her greatest fear head on. She needed him by her side to know that everything would not be as she had feared. Esmeralda just needed to hear Eddie's voice to help calm her down.

Although she needed her husband, she would not dare share this news over the phone, though. She would unfortunately need to exercise patience and wait until he got home later that evening. She needed to be held by her husband at that moment. Entangled in her emotions she desperately wished she could cry it all away.

Evening could not come any sooner for Esmeralda, Jeanette or Darryl. Everyone was on edge as anticipation boiled them alive. Eddie got home. Esmeralda took him to their bedroom where she planned to break the news or so she thought. To her surprise he was not as shocked nor nervous as she was.

He admitted that he already knew this day would come. He had expected her life to play out this way but secretly prayed it wouldn't. How can one expect to play with bees and not get stung? Or play with fire and not get burned? Or walk on glass and not get cut? The outcome was predictable. From where he stood, it was simple and not nearly as complicated as Esmeralda's frantic face made it out to be.

Eddie's life led him up to this very point. Difficult times were not foreign to him. He was, in a way, built for the powerful punches that attempted to take him out. He was a fighter and would not allow him nor his family to go down. He collected his thoughts as they were not all scattered and entangled as Esmeralda's worries vomited through her lips.

He sat Esmeralda down and began to lay out the plan. Esmeralda was without words as she heard her dear husband lay out a plan to help position Jeanette to finish school. Anger and sadness swirled like a tornado within her heart. She couldn't believe that Eddie was not going to force Jeanette to marry Darryl. Their Catholic beliefs pointed in this very direction! "Who would they be if not hypocrites to have her unmarried and pregnant," she wrestled within. She was even more surprised to hear of the financial support he would offer.

Esmeralda spoke her mind in certain areas and he brought her to a place of understanding. He caused her to see things from a different angle. Not the angle of others looking in, but of her as her mom caring for her daughter. He gave her perspective. It was not easy for Eddie to lead her there.

Esmeralda did not have a healthy relationship with her daughter. They fought over everything and anything. They just couldn't see eye-to-eye. It was difficult to love her as Jeanette's verbal punches would leave her emotionally wounded. She sobbed in Eddie's arms that day as she beat herself up for not being the mom Jeanette needed. She did her best, but this moment was just another reminder that her best was just not good enough. She felt weak in the knees when Eddie motioned that it's time to face both Jeanette and Darryl.

Chapter 4

NOT ALL MEXICANS CAN COOK

Jeanette left her parents room confused. She couldn't understand that out of all her disapproving behavior, that this situation seemed to have brought her more respect from her parents. It just didn't make sense. She expected to be kicked out and on her own to figure life out, but instead, it appeared that her parents were loving her through this. She didn't recognize this type of behavior. She knew love as a child, but as a teenager, she just couldn't be enough for them.

At fifteen, she concluded that she was just not going to be good enough for them, no matter what she attempted. They wanted more from her and she was not willing to be molded into the image they wanted. She was not their perfect Mexican daughter. She didn't even know how to cook. Mexicans are known for cooking and feeding people for no reason at all. They are known to always have food ready to offer guests even when guests are not hungry at all. She was not what they wanted from a daughter and this moment proved it in the worst possible way.

Jeanette's head hung low on her way to her room that night. Low due to humility, but also low due to shame. She shamed her parents. They fought many obstacles to be able to provide a life in the United States. They sacrificially lived a life of lack so their daughters could have a successful future. They gave up their business and homes in Mexico so Jeanette could have an education without living in a corrupted country. They had great plans for Jeanette's future and here it was dismantled. Jeanette's future was now destroyed.

Entering her senior year of high school pregnant held more challenges than Jeanette had anticipated. Not only were students' whispers evident, but her teachers now pitied her. Their faces spoke so loudly of their thoughts that she threw her life away. Even so, with the funny looks her way, the pregnancy progressed at what seemed to be a fast rate. Jeanette used her invisible powers to tune out the noise and focused on her academics.

Mixed emotions would at times fog her mind. She questioned if this new level of determination was necessary. Afterall, how could she continue school once the baby was born? "I will be a high school drop out anyway, right?" she battled internally. Still, she was intentional not to quit as the days increased in difficulty. Sleepy-eyed and drained from energy was now the new norm. After school naps had become a new tradition. She was lost without them.

Without her rest, exhaustion would cause her mouth to shoot fiery darts and take jabs at Darryl. Before her pregnancy she attacked Darryl, now her inability to control her moodiness was unbearable for him to stand by and undergo such abuse. Darryl expected difficulties, but he was astonished at the new level of torment he was enduring. He was not sure if he had it in him to continue.

Although things were intense, there came yet another level of hardship. The desire to be loved increased and Jeanette desperately wanted her and Darryl's relationship to work out. She had painted this picture in her mind of how they would live happily ever after. This illusion was just that though–an illusion. It was all in her head and not the reality. The fighting became more hostile and during one fight Darryl punched a hole through her bedroom wall. He would yell; she would yell back. She would use words to cut him and he would return the hate. He would leave and she would sob. She spent many days and nights merely comforted by the pillow that absorbed her storm-like tears of anguish.

The pain of rejection was unbearable and excruciating. Many times, Darryl just couldn't take another heart-slicing word from Jeanette. It was now the norm to run away and let her be. He didn't want anything to do with her and her razor sharp words. The punctures were striking deeper and deeper beyond repair. The pain of rejection was unbearable and excruciating.

There was very little understanding of the requirements needed for a relationship to survive. They did not know that relationships need more than the feelings of love to exist. Relationships need love in action. They said they loved each other and yet their behavior displayed hate. Their relationship was headed in the wrong direction. It was barely surviving. It was hanging on by a thread. Using the word "love" was their thread and it was tearing and splitting with every passing moment.

Although the word love is a noun, it is also a verb. Love is a decision; an action. It must be walked out and displayed daily. Love in action would mean Jeanette would be in the process of walking out or achieving a decision made. Feelings will come and feelings will go, but the decision to love must remain regardless of the feelings they each felt during the difficult moments.

Without this vital information, Jeanette was lost in her emotions.Unknowingly misunderstanding love and lust. She was unaware that love is a verb. So she spent most of her pregnancy in tears.

Before pregnancy, Jeanette battled an eating disorder. To see her body enlarging affected her self image even more. To top it off Darryl's betrayal and infidelity caused her to feel the worst level of rejection. This fantasy that they were meant for each other was fading faster than she could hold on to. The pregnancy was full of dark moments where Jeanette wished she had the strength to crash her car into a pole or tree and be released from the torment of rejection.

The lies and deceptions ate at her self esteem. She now believed the lie that she was not enough. She was not enough for Darryl and that was the reason he sought after other girls. She couldn't meet his needs or wants. With this rejection evident every time she caught him in a lie, she pushed him further away in hopes to protect her aching heart.

She hated feeling so alone. It was almost at times more tortuous than his insults and betrayal. Darryl would be sorrowful and ask for forgiveness. Jeanette would accept his apology. Things would be okay for a couple of days, until they weren't–until one of them treated the other like garbage with words and actions to display their bitterness and displeasure. This cycle continued. They attempted to mask their pain, but it was becoming more and more unmanageable to contain.

This pain and sadness that was being transfigured into anger was coming to its end. Although they both hid their pain by shielding it with anger, it was only a shield. This anger in its deepest foundational form was still sadness. Jeanette was deceiving herself into thinking sadness didn't dwell in her heart. Darryl was deceiving himself into thinking he was stronger than pain. Hiding pain was his way of combating it from surfacing and revealing his vulnerability. He thought suffocated hidden pain was unable to breathe nor live which meant he was in control. Deceived by their lies to themselves and each other, they continued the whirlwind pattern toward their destruction.

During those anguish-filled moments, Jeanette's inability to think clearly disoriented her. Suffering from heartache, she questioned her ability to be the mom this forming baby needed and deserved. "Can I really do this? Can I really be a single teen mom?" she questioned. She fought the internal voices of hate and love for her baby's dad. She refused to allow sadness to sneak in, invade and cram her heart. She fought to remember the reason she embarked on this journey into parenthood. Her amnesia-stricken mind could not find the memory through the swarm of emotions that entangled and choked her heart.

On a night filled with the familiar anguish, Jeannette wrote a poem as she often would to release pent up emotions. Her poem writing days traced as far back as she could remember. Writing poems was her way of expressing all her hidden feelings. Verbally expressing them made her feel weak, yet in writing, she could both attach herself and distance herself from those emotions.

Without a Word

Unrecognizable faces walk without saying one word
I'm waiting for my name to be said; to be heard

Silence is golden, but for me it is petrifying
I don't know if I'm being born or if I'm dying

I hear screaming,
I don't know from where & I don't know why
I see them.
They're here for me, but without a word they just cry
Is there something wrong? What's going on?
All of a sudden I see nothing' nothing but the sun

I don't know where I am, or where I'm being led to
Someone is walking with me and holding my hand, but who?
This has to be a dream of some kind
But the exit is something I can't find

One dark and rainy night on her way home from work while listening to songs that unknowingly fed sadness, Jeanette led herself down a disastrous thought. She gripped the steering wheel as rain smeared on her windshield. The windshield wipers danced ferociously to keep up with the falling rain. Sobbingly she screamed in terror-filled anger at the thought of continuing to live this life. Her petrified screams roared from her lungs only to bounce back at her without a single soul knowing the pain and despair she was in.

Darryl's deceptions continued to eat at her. Frightened by his inability to love her, she was terrified of their future together. "Even if I left him," she argued. "He would still need to be very much part of my life," she debated within herself. "Darryl would always be your baby's father," was the pounding phrase she could hear in her mom's voice. That phrase had become her mom's new motto in hopes to support both Darryl and Jeanette. Whether she liked it or not, Jeanette would need to continue a life with Darryl in one capacity or another.

Coparenting with a malicious and deceptive person caused her thoughts to race toward her baby's 5th birthday, then his 10th, then 16th. "Who would this sweet child end up to be if she continued this path?" She managed to say to herself. She feared her precious child would be consumed by her darkness and Darryl's anger. Who knows what type of monster Darryl and her would create through the dysfunctional relationship. She gripped the steering wheel a grain tighter. Bracing for the impact, she could in a glimpse, see herself accelerating and ramming into the pole head first.

She blinked. She attempted to catch her breath. She felt heat flood her whole body. Weight was pressing on her chest making it difficult to breath and think. She blinked. She breathed. She looked. She saw her surroundings. In panic, she shook her head and screamed. She shook her head as if to wake herself up from the nightmare. Yelling, she cried out for help. She gripped the steering wheel as tight as her hands could bear. Within seconds, she shook herself out of her thoughts. She knew she could not go through with ending her and her baby's life.

She sobbed intensively through her entire drive home. As overwhelming as that moment was, it cracked her once fortified castle. That moment allowed for a speck of light to enter her dark mansion of pain. Thankful for whatever helped her escape her thoughts of suicide, she weeped at the end of her street. No matter the difficultness of the situation with Darryl, she knew death was not her answer. Although she wished it would be, in irritation, she was reminded that if she went through with it, he would win.

That day, she found a new reason to fight for her life. She was not about to let him get the best of her. She would not allow herself to be consumed by the darkness. Light overpowers darkness. No matter how dark it is; light cannot be consumed by darkness. Somehow she felt a glimpse of light. The light, as unstable as it was, was her way of pressing forward. Derangely, her pride took over and she committed to herself that she would not give Darryl this win. She would fight. She would fight for her son.

The time came to give birth. On May 1st, 2001 at 9:30pm, Zaqry Keith Lanier was born by emergency C-Section. By then, Darryl had come back around or so it seemed, again. Darryl waited anxiously outside the delivery room waiting for his first child to be brought out to him. Full of uncontained emotions he released them all out. Angry that Jeanette requested no one to hold him until she did, brought his blood to boil. He was forced to let anger have its way by kicking the doors and waiting room wall to vocalize his disagreement to her decision. Jeanette was still under full anesthesia while the nurse bathed Zaqry. Darryl was forced to watch in agony.

As Jeanette began to wake up from the anesthesia, she began crying hysterically. Nurses came to her aid only to find out she was not in physical pain. They learned of her situation and her dilemma to go back to school and obtain her diploma so late into the year. "The C-section recovery will take weeks to heal," she cried. The nurse closest to her attempted to pacify her misery, but Jeanette's reality sank in. She could not contain the tears and sorrow that filled her heart knowing she would be a highschool dropout leaving her parents' sacrifices behind. "High school dropouts can't get a job!", she cried, defeatedly. Her mom rushed in to console her as soon as she heard of Jeanette's panic-attack. Her mom and nurse did what they could to console Jeanette until she finally wore herself out and began to once again breathe slowly.

In that moment compassion filled Esmeralda's heart for her daughter. It brought her back to the times Jeanette needed love and support through her scraped knees or bee sting pain. She held her daughter with the intent to march down to the superintendent's office and find a solution to Jeanette's dilemma. She had never felt this foreign feeling of bravery rise up within her. She was determined to find a solution regardless of the cost.

Up until that moment confronting English speaking people caused such intimidation. Her broken English had been getting the best of her. Until now! She knew she would find a way for her daughter to obtain her high school diploma.

Once cleared from the anesthesia, with near swollen-shut and tear-filled eyes, Jeanette layed eyes on her baby for the first time. Zaqry was the most perfect baby she had ever seen. He was perfect in every way possible. Holding him made every inch of pain go away instantly. Jeanette felt like the luckiest person to ever walk this earth. While looking at his amazing beautiful face, everything that made her sad disappeared without a trace. There she laid, looking at him, thinking of what his future would hold. In that moment of admiration, she decided that she knew of at least one thing on what Zaqry's future held; it was her. Determined, she promised she would do everything in her power to be beside him forever.

Throughout the many difficult moments in determining which decision of the three to make, Jeanette was unaware that she could be confronted with joy. Joy was found in Zaqry; within her new life as his mom. Joy had the ability to overpower anger, sadness and pain all at the same time. Hopeful of their future, peace began to sneak into her heart. She took a deep breath and held her baby close as she rested in this new found joy.

Chapter 5

THE BEGINNING AGAIN

Wearing her cap and gown, Jeanette walked down the stage in June of 2001 to receive her high school diploma from Fullerton Union High School. This diploma came from the days and nights of reading and filling out homework packets while simultaneously having Zaqry latched to her during his feedings. As Jeanette sat back down and staring at her diploma cover, gratitude filled her heart. This diploma came to her reach due to a large number of people supporting her decision to keep Zaqry.

With heartfelt gratitude, she was reminded of her school caseworker's love, who noticed her inability to stand up and sent her to the ER so doctors could patch the liquid leaking out of her spine. Thankful for her teachers who valued life and loved her through her distress, she acknowledged their participation in this achievement. This victory did not come without overwhelming gratitude for her parents, specifically her mom who fought and advocated for her so she could be at that ceremony that day. That moment was held together by a powerful feeling of gratitude that embraced and surrounded Jeanette.

Photos were taken as smiles around her beamed from camera to camera. For that moment, the girls around her that once triggered jealousy had no effect on her. These girls, with Darryl's flirtatious behavior, once had the power to provoke her to jealousy. Today, neither Jeanette nor Darryl set each other up for failure. Relieved, she did not have to see their faces any longer, she hugged Darryl and smiled at the camera again.

Darryl's smile was hiding his regret of dropping out of high school. He was rejoicing with Jeanette in her accomplishment but was beating himself up for not continuing his education and wearing that cap and gown alongside her. Resentment for being the one needing to provide financially for their son began to silently slither into his heart. He observed Jeanette's family with balloons and flowers hugging her and wished he could experience that feeling of accomplishment, appreciation, and recognition. Once home, he closed his eyes to rest from the regret of allowing himself to be a statistic.

Darryl and Jeanette tried to make things work for the first year of Zaqry's life, but the game they played was increasing in intensity. This increase resulted in the enlarged compounded severity of the unforgivable wounds. Darryl would surround himself with girls he was attracted to which caused Jeanette's jealous heart to desire revenge. She knew how to play this game. She knew what buttons to push. She knew what brought him back to his knees for her heart. Sadness had a key to Jeanette's heart every time she thought she got to Darryl. She understood that the reason for his anger was solely due to the fact that he could not have her. It was unfortunate that he didn't know what to do when he did have her. Mishandling each other's hearts was a game that turned into a tournament for both.

A year of living together caused dreadful damage and they couldn't find a way to make things work. It was torturous for both. It was evident they were running low on what they needed to make it work. While playing the game, Jeanette began seeking comfort from other guys. Darryl's heart too was no longer desiring to connect with her and preferred to find connection with the beautiful girls at work. The lack of sleep from feedings and diaper changes brought them to a greater inability to care for each other's tender hearts started coming to an end.

On November 9th 2001, a few weeks shy of Jeanette's eighteenth birthday, she wrote another poem in her sleepless night as she worried about what Darryl was doing. Her confusing state made it difficult to navigate the direction to take. She knew things with Darryl were becoming more and more difficult to manage and yet she loved him. Although this love she held for him appeared to be real, she was veering off course. She was teetering off a cliff in hopes to jump to a safer side.

Jeanette was in desperate search to feel loved, wanted, and accepted. Darryl's ability to disregard her heart and intentionally take girls to work and be there for them was tearing Jeanette's heart and causing scar tissue to callus around her heart. She desperately desired love yet found herself more and more lonely. Again, poem writing became her outlet.

Where is the nervously heart-pounding soul
Did it drift away or did it just fall?

Was it lost through the exchange of a promise that was meant to be?
Or should the truth be out so we can both see?

The feelings I hold inside are trapped within my heart
I want to let them free, but that means we'd have to part

I now nor ever want to be afraid
But it was my love for you that I had to trade

I do not regret for what I have done
I will face the facts, I will not run

There is a moment & time for everything; and here's mine
I've been approached by a sign

So I take a breath and hope you're not sad
Because I lost the love for you I once had

On February 15, 2002, through tear-filled eyes and the familiar anguish and confusion, Jeannette layed in bed with her paper and pen. Her pen flowed freely as her heart choked the words from coming forth her lips. Her lips couldn't utter the words through the lodging in her throat, but the pen continued to capture her misery.

The Truth To Face

Down the river fast and steady
Went our love without being ready
Frightened & scared with no one around
Was our lost love, that cannot be found

Ruined and torn was my heart at the end
It's just a shame you could not be my friend
I am lonely and scared without you by my side
But the truth from me you tried to hide

I thought we were one, I thought we were it
But how the pieces of this puzzle just don't seem to fit

Where I am going and who I will be
Is not up to us, it's just up to me
Over the rainbow, under the sea
This is hard to know but in silence we'll be

Done With

A forceful power full of joy
You have taken and will destroy
Up the ladder, down the slide
Is the game you played and tried to hide
To hell with you, we are done
We weren't mutually having fun
Away with stress, away with you
This relationship you just blew

Hard to deal with, yes I am
All you say to me is "God damn!"
Life has its rains, winds and storms
Our love was all appearance, never showing all its forms

Jeanette finally fell asleep on her mascara smeared pillow and braced for what tomorrow would bring. The next day was filled with the residue from yesterday. As dust settles, it doesn't disappear, it remains on sight latching on to everything it lands on. Settled dust is helpful still, Jeanette can see with a clearer perspective. She could see what she was approaching. This time she would not run, but instead she would face it. This time she would not ignore it. This time she would not sweep it under the rug. This time she promised herself she would be different. This time she *was* different. She was ready for the storms up ahead.

The next few weeks looked similar to her last. She was still caring for Zaqry, going to the community college, and working at H&R Block along with her side gig of being an extra in movies and sitcoms. She was determined to be happy. She was determined to be what she knew Zaqry needed from her. Zaqry needed both his mom and dad together.

Although she conjured everything within her to make this their reality, it was becoming more and more difficult each time a young man, during Hollywood filmings, would give her attention. Her heart was slowly yet quickly becoming out of reach for Darryl. He couldn't woo her the way these guys were doing. He knew her. He knew the pain and damage she could cause with her sweet and beautiful lips. He continued to stay his distance and regretted his disengagement more and more each time. But regret was not larger than his fear of enduring more pain. For now, regret was distant and not at all in its full potential.

Nothing had changed within Darryl and Jeanette's relationship. Darryl continued to lie, deceive, manipulate and gaslight Jeanette. Jeanette continued to hide her pain with anger and belittle Darryl while allowing herself to be entranced by the other young men in her life. Darryl and Jeanette continued to respond out of pain and use their anger-filled words as their source of ammunition against one another. Nothing had changed and yet through their suffering, everything had.

On April 11, 2002, less than a month shy of Zaqry's 1st birthday, Jeanette wrote:

Rain pouring hard down my face
I look to find it only in my space

It is not gloomy or sad for all, just me
It's such a confusing thought, how could this be

I'm scared, lonely in the dark
He left me wounded, leaving a mark
Abandoned with no one in sight
In a dark black place without any light

I trapped myself without breathing room
Without that light I will be doomed

How do I get out? How will I be free?
It was his fault, he ruined me!

Jeanette was becoming more and more aware of the slow death she was embracing. The gaslighting was causing her to feel crazy as if she didn't understand up from down or left from right. Darryl would dance around his words, enclosing Jeanette with his lies. Jeanette wondered if she was becoming deranged as she tried to detangle his lies to find the truth only to find herself intertwined and trapped in them. Her predicament could not have been new to the world. "Surely there were others who had faced similar situations," she thought. And yet, she didn't know who to go to. Where could she find the help she needed? She continued to find comfort within her paper and pen.

My Calamity

As time stands still, I see things more clear
With every passing thought, it becomes to get real
No running around all over the place
I just sit here determining my next phase

No one around me, I'm here by myself
Each memory now organized & on it's own shelf
No one understands me, and what I've been through
I guess it's the price to pay for what is now due

I am alone by myself with a child in my arms
And no matter what, this child will be without harm
The outside world awaits us & we're glad to be received
And yet, people will criticize & believe what they want to believe

Tears run down my face, at the thought of my calamity
Fears run through my heart of the problem & its longevity
People without worries complain about nothing
But I am always complaining about everything!
Why can't I be happy ? Why can't I be free?
Why is it so difficult for us to just agree?

The world may turn and spin for years to come
But my time spinning with the Darryl seems to be done
There's no time to waste, I'll get started right now
My only problem is I just don't know how

Jeanette continued to wrestle with the decision to stay with Darryl or to leave him. She felt herself being pulled further and further away by the thought of the other young men now in her life. She was intrigued and was nearing the trap of their bait. With her faint Catholic upbringing, she knew she should stay, marry Darryl, and stick this out with him. She saw it as her punishment for having sinned. Although she knew of this distant God, she just couldn't bear the pain any longer and would continue writing poems to try to sort through her feelings.

At Zaqry's 1st birthday party, Jeanette disregarded Darryl's request one too many times. All he wanted was for her to stay at the party with all the guests. The 100+ acre park where they rented a sheltered picnic area offered plenty of amenities to all. Guests could go on the trail, playground, baseball fields, hiking, fishing, and much more. Instead of wanting to mingle and have small talk with the guests, Jeanette sought independence to venture out to the basketball court with her friends. Her 18 year old mind was still adjusting to the responsibilities of being a mom. Her refusal to be controlled led to the biggest fight in the history of their relationship.

Frustration began to fill Darryl's body. His heart began to race. Anger filled his face. His flushed and rosy complexion was evident to all. Darryl's anger got the best of him and he vomited out words that he could never take back. He made all the guests aware of what he thought of Jeanette. He told them details about her past moments of infidelity. She stood in shock while he berated and exposed her.

Darryl began to describe what he envisioned her times with other young men were like. She now felt completely and utterly naked in front of all those that came to celebrate Zaqry's life. She did not know how to defend herself from his family and friends. He was right. She had done all those things. She was embarrassed. Shame gripped her and her throat closed up. Darryl's description of her behavior made the guest uncomfortable, but this young man needed to release all the pent up emotions he had. An explosion of anger-filled words penetrated the air that day. He was hurting too. He had been hurting for sometime now. He was just as confused at his love and hate for this girl as she was about him.

He too was trying to make sense of the mess they were in. He was provoked. Jeanette carelessly mishandled his delicate heart one too many times. He was not going to admit his heart was tender and delicate though. It was best to ram her down like football practices taught him to do. He shredded her with his words. He was sick and tired of being mistreated.

Jeanette selfishly overlooked his feelings one too many times. No matter how often he tried to love her, she pushed him away. He had grown weary of being disregarded. He didn't know how to show another emotion except for anger that day. He too had learned how to self protect. He had lived life long enough to know it required survival instincts to come out of this alive.

This young man, 19 now, needed to feel heard. He had felt invisible to her. She wouldn't seem to consider his ideas and would shoot him down without the opportunities to dream with her. That day her monster, Control, rose up against his monster, Anger. The battle was brutal and they each intended to win.

Growing up the middle child to a broken home, Darryl experienced his superpower of invisibility too. Parents aren't supposed to forget their child's birthdays, but some parents do. Parents are supposed to show love and support at their child's endeavors, but some don't. Darryl held on to vivid memories of being forgotten, overlooked, and ignored. Happy Little League memories of accomplishments are overshadowed by the memories of his parents not present cheering him on.

He would get dropped off week after week for both practices and games. His parents didn't stay to watch him practice and improve his skills. They didn't attend his games to watch his home runs. They were not there to partake in his victories or encourage him through the defeats. The lack of his parents' presence along with Jeanette's neglect to care for his heart created such devastation within his once tender heart. Jeanette's disregard to his feelings and his desire to make that special day magical ignited his eruption.

Jeanette's family and friends had compassion for

her. One of her co-workers hugged her as she weeped in humiliation. She had worked so hard for her son's 1st birthday party. It was now awkward for guests so they left before the party festivities even began. Their son's birthday was definitely memorable; it was just not the type of memories they had wished to have created.

Jeanette's need for control created monsters of them both. Her need to dominate in fear that she would be dominated herself brought her to this very place. Jeanette was driven by her mind which held a picture of her grandmother. She was not about to end up like her; full of bitterness and resentment for staying married to a man who mistreated her.

Fear was the underlying cause of her behavior. Fear that she would be trapped brought forth enraged savages of them both. No longer could they hold back the pain and anger from demolishing what was once a sweet high school romance.

Ferociously determined to win, they each slashed one another with words. But this day was destined to come. It was no longer on the horizon. It was here. That day, they both put a stop to the torturous relationship. They both left the park wounded and defeated.

Song of Solomon 2:15 talks about catching the little foxes for the little foxes spoil the vine. Darryl and Jeanette's relationship was made up of multiple little moments that shaped their future. Along with other decisions, the decision to purposely make each other jealous were the little foxes that were let loose and ended up spoiling the field of love in their relationship.

Jealousy was not the only culprit for the ending of their relationship, though. Selfishness, jumping to conclusions, immaturity, lack of communication skills, not setting up boundaries, and not discussing their feelings with each other was what led to the mistrust, dishonesty, disrespect, and lack of loyalty that led to their broken relationship. Their once-tender hearts became callused and hardened through the various combinations of culprits forming against them.

Similar to the domino effect, their relationship was being formed by one decision after another. Each decision not only affected them as a couple, but these decisions affected the next option of decisions to be made. They were in a cycle of dysfunctional behavior. Because they bottled up their true feelings and did not share them with each other, they kept each other in the dark about a lot of things that had the potential to be resolved or even prevented had they just let down their guards and let each other in. While in this self-preservation mode, they searched for other sources to fulfill their needs which led them both to be unfaithful to each other and hence evitable the separation in the park.

Chapter 6

THE TOXIC RELATIONSHIP

May 1st, 2002 marked the beginning of the inconsistent and fluctuating confusion this little family of three would endure. That day as she saw Darryl pack up his things and leave, Jeanette's heart wrestled with her mind. Tug-of-war is only fun when playing with people and a rope, not pleasant when it is with her mind and heart. She is one and the same. No matter which wins, she loses. Her mind knew better than to allow her to endure the continual hostility and rejection. Her heart desperately wanted to love and be loved.

The days turned to weeks and the weeks turned to months. Confused at the storm of emotions abrasively colliding with each other, Jeanette picked up her pen to write.

8/4/2002

I will proceed on striving to achieve
I will give back on what I have received
Life will never be as planned
But if I fall, on my feet, I will land
I do not regret what has been done
I will not regret what the future will become
There is no limit, I will reach; reach for that star
It will be a long journey and it will be far
I will not give up, stop, or break
Because my future is at stake

Through this confusing time, she felt led to write Darryl a letter. A letter intended for Darryl and yet not intended for his eyes to read. A letter she would never give him, but a letter to help her through her process of confusion and grief from their recent encounter and sleeping with each other again. She couldn't understand why it happened or where this relationship was headed. This letter was her attempt to find a way to form a window to bring light to her dark mansion.

Dearest Darryl, 8/8/02

This letter is meant to express my feelings towards everything going on between us. (the "us" I want). I'm not sure how to start, but I'm pretty sure I've told you already that I cannot emotionally handle most things.

Right now I'm totally confused about what went on

Sunday, Monday, and Tuesday. I don't know if it meant anything to you or not, but anything that happens between you and I means a lot to me (even the arguments that I want to forget).

I was talking to my grandma and grandpa and both think that I'm suffering. I don't think that they're correct, but in a sense I guess I am, because I miss you so very extremely much.

My grandma especially keeps wanting me to beg you back. I have no problem with begging (but I know you hate it). She wants me to be back with you for the wrong reasons (in my eyes). Since financially she was not stable, that's all she wants for me. She doesn't want Zaqry suffering with anything having to do with money or materialistic things.

Yeah, life doesn't revolve around all that, but for people that didn't have it, it does. The reason I'm telling you all this is because if someone tries to tell you to take me back for Zaqry's sake, please don't do it.

If I am taken back I don't want it to be out of kindness or pity. So just so you know I would so very much love to be with you, but only if it is completely and fully together.

And another thing on what I said about regretting sleeping with you. My emotions were talking. I told you I get extremely emotional. I'm sure we slept with each other for a reason, I just hope the reason was mutual, if not then there's something else in my life I have to worry about at night.

Another thing, what you said about me not being a good mother, that really really hurt. You're the only person that can say anything and I'll feel it. I just hope you didn't really mean it and if you did then I only hope it was the spur of the moment of being really angry at me. Well there's more to write, but I didn't feel comfortable telling you the rest right now, I'm just afraid.

Your (desired to be) friend,

Jeanette

PS. I LOVE U

PPS Even if I don't show it

Three days later, Jeanette found herself yet again, alone in her ill-lit and gloomy castle. As she stares off into the distance she tries to make sense of her life and all the emotions tied into it. Zaqry was in bed sleeping as she picked up her notebook to release her pent up emotions.

8/11/02

Quietly I wonder what life holds for me
How will I stand and who will I be
So many possibilities I hold in my hand
But with all these distractions how will I land
Mistakes I will make and know I will do
But I will not repeat the old and make new
Temptations will come and I will ignore
My surroundings are enough, I will not want more
Treasure day by day;do not wander too far
But I will always keep reaching for that one star

Struggling with the shame of her betrayal toward Darryl she remembered a memory in disgust. The passionate embrace and kisses toward the other young man made her stomach churn that moment. Again, in her distraught state, she picked up her pen and allowed her thoughts to breathe words onto that paper.

8/18/02

Things between us didn't work out
Because we would always scream and shout
Nevertheless, our love is still strong
But it was me who did you wrong

I still love you and I still care
But the heart breaking I can't bare
I know it was me; I am to blame
And my heart right now is full of shame
Painful stabs in the heart I just made
And the consequences will get paid

But you are strong and will get by
There won't be a tear left to cry
Tough and strong you will stay
The loss for you I will pay

Dear Darryl, 8/18/02

I would like to start out by apologizing for my words and actions. They were very b*tch* and I understand why things aren't working out for us. It's me.

The reason for this letter (and I know I'll want to regret it later) is to express my feelings. I can't really do that verbally with you, because you talk back. Anyway, right now at this point of my life, I don't have hope for us. That doesn't mean I don't want to be with you, or marry you or be the mama for your babies, it just means that the way things are going right now between us. I don't see ourselves together.

And another thing, if things change (which I doubt) and we actually work things out, I will not be able to fully and truly be with you as long as I live here. I don't know how I will do it, but I will move away. It will be extremely hard and difficult for me as well as for Zaqry, but it is something I must do in order to be satisfied (or at least that's the way I see it right now).

You probably won't get this letter just like all the other letters I write to you. But even though you don't know all this, it still feels good to express my thoughts and feelings. And just so you know I love you still and with every minute that goes by I miss you more and my love for you thickens even more.

always,

Jeanette

Jeanette kept all these things to herself and set in motion taking one day at a time knowing that is the only way to proceed. She would not allow herself to get lost in the fantasy of tomorrow or in the burdensomes of yesterday. She established her plan to only focus on today; day after day.

After confusion began to disintegrate and fizzle out, at one point Darryl became Jeanette's booty call. She called on him during those lonely nights that she needed to be held. Darryl gladly accepted her invitations of uncommitted sex. He sinisterly enjoyed knowing that he was the one she was calling upon. They walked this unhealthy yet satisfying approach of misleading each other.

During certain moments they each individually thought there was potential for reconciliation only to find they were being deceived. They were not ready to embark on life with their hearts attached to one another. They didn't know how to run a three legged race and were done tripping and falling onto the floor's abrasive and rugged surface.

After about a year of living on their own, both Jeanette and Darryl were managing coparenting as best they knew how. Jeanette would allow visitations based on her mood towards Darryl. There were times she did and other times that her manipulation would unleash to new heights. Little did she know the impact prohibiting those father and son moments would cause. She didn't care though, she just didn't want Darryl winning all the time. He was off to a carefree life while she was set to fulfill her commitments.

Darryl lived in the best neighborhood his limited paycheck could afford. In fear of Zaqry's safety, time and time again Jeanette suggested other meeting options, but Darryl's desire to have him over his apartment ruled out other options.

One night after her evening shift at the hotel where she worked, Jeanette dashed to his place in hopes both she and Zaqry could get through his neighborhood before midnight. Fear struck her when she couldn't get into the small gated complex. She was outside the gates surrounded by dark shadows and cars slowly cruising by. With eyes looking at her young female body, she panicked as she redialed Darryl's phone number.

"Pick up, pick up, pick up!" her mind cried out. No answer. In desperation, she looked at her surroundings again. There was little hope that she could make her way back to her car without someone catcalling her or worse approaching her. She redialed. No answer. Nervously, she redialed yet again. He answered! He came down with Zaqry. Darryl couldn't quite figure Jeanette out, but understood her face and walked her to her car. Zaqry continued to be tossed back and forth through visitations with his separated parents.

During one of the tossings to Darryl, Darryl found himself in great fear similar to Jeanette's. While Jeanette continued to take half his paycheck, surviving came through his side hustle, drug selling. That was the only solution he could obtain in order to make ends meet. Through his sale transactions he would at times smoke a small part of the stash of weed with his clients.

Immediately after completing a sale and a smoke session, Jeanette pulled up to drop off Zaqry. He took Zaqry quickly and went into his apartment so Jeanette wouldn't notice his bloodshot eyes. Fear struck him as he stared at Zaqry while closing the door behind him. "Oh no! I'm just like my parents!" was the thought that hammered within his mind.

Darryl began gulping glass after glass of water in hopes to flush things out of his system at a faster pace. In coming to his senses, he thought "How can I do to Zaqry the very thing I hated that was done to me?!" The realization that he was becoming his parents formed knots to his stomach. He was on a mission to down as much water as possible to help him come down his high.

The fear of becoming his parents was continually pounding his mind as he attempted to distract himself and play peek-a-boo with his son. That pivotal moment changed his trajectory as a father. He vowed in his heart to never be high around Zaqry again.

As Darryl and Jeanette continued to live their separate lives, Darryl went to visit his biological mom and step-dad. His step-dad was known as "dad" to Darryl his whole life. Darryl only visited his biological father, Richard, during his summers. His plan was only to visit his parents, but his roommate had other plans and ransacked Darryl's room in search of drugs and money. Darryl's landlord called

Darryl with the shocking and unpleasant news. This destructive behavior from Darryl's roommate left the landlord with no choice. Darryl was evicted as well.

From the conversation, Darryl understood what items were left and told his landlord to just donate them. Darryl was no stranger to not having belongings to his name. He knew not to attach himself to possessions as they can vanish at any moment. This situation left Darryl homeless. What seemed to have been a visit to northern California, turned out to be much more. November of 2003 Darryl unknowingly relocated himself over 500 miles north of his son.

Darryl continued to be forced to pay child support and saw his paychecks dwindle down to barely anything. He reverted back to what he knew would bring easy money. He began his new source of income by selling drugs again. Selling was a simple thing for him. It was as if it came naturally to deal and work with people who lived this lifestyle.

This particular lifestyle was what he'd known growing up. There had been different people staying in his house as his parents tried to help them. If it was not their addictive behaviors, it was their need for a place to live that brought them to board in their house. Sharing his bedroom became customary in his household. Moving from one place to another was also part of his childhood. People drinking, smoking and doing much more was more familiar than he understood it should have been. The yelling, screaming, and physical fighting was also just part of life. At least now, he could control it more. He would be the one doing the punching, drinking and cussing this time around. He would now have a voice in what and who he would allow in his life.

In all the grinding and chasing the dollar, Darryl dated different girls. Although they offered what he was searching for, there was still a void. They were not Jeanette. As soon as he felt like he could see himself spending more time with particular girls, he was intentional to let them know the hard truth of his life; he was a dad. While on dates, the harsh statement flowed freely from his mouth and slapped girls in the face: "If I ever get the chance to get Jeanette and Zaqry back, I will." Some young ladies didn't see room in his heart for them, so at some point their relationship with him would end. All left, except for one.

This particular young lady took pride in her ability to charm him away from thoughts of Jeanette. She accepted the challenge. Over time, he found refuge in the arms of this young woman who made him feel like he was her everything. She valued and respected him. She laughed at his silly jokes. She bathed him with her love. She accepted him for who he was and he felt her care for him, but she had her own demons.

She was great to him only when she was sober. That seemed to be the only downfall with his girlfriend and friends; they would act foolishly after so many drinks. And yet, this is the life he signed up for. This is the life he knew. He didn't see it getting too far better than this. Yet, he still had aspirations of making this path better, though. He dreamed of one day owning his own home, working, and enjoying all life had to offer.

Chapter 7

TUG -OF-WAR

At 20, Jeanette found herself in search of more than what life had been offering. Although she loved her new role as a mom, she still felt the familiar void. "What could be missing?" were her constant thoughts. She was determined to find a more fulfilling life than the day-to-day grind that came from work, school, and motherhood.

One day her friend from high school invited her to church. She was hesitant about Christianity for she remembered attending church with Darryl and his foster family once. People in the congregation were singing with hands raised as if worshiping this God of the Bible. That was foreign to her. Her Catholic Mass was not filled with people doing such things. Reluctantly, she accepted the invitation from her friend, Anna.

Jeanette found herself hungry to know more about this God the Bible talks about and continued to go back to that church. Jeanette met God at Seeker's Chapel in Anaheim, California. This encounter was fascinating and beautiful. She grew up going occasionally to church and hearing about God, but never experiencing this great love that Christians spoke about. She didn't know very many Christians who walked a life that was evident of their faith except for Darryl's previous foster parents.

In confusion, she showed up at their house, one day unannounced, full of questions about her new found faith in Jesus Christ. Lacking knowledge of truth, she was in wonder hearing about a purpose filled life. She didn't know she had a purpose and was eager to learn more about it. They gave her some resources to read and listen to. They set up weekly meetings so she could be mentored by Darryl's previous foster mom, Michelle.

Michelle walked her through the books of the Bible, teaching her of the history of the formation of the Bible and the early church. They began a reading plan where they would read together and discuss it. The Bible had always seemed boring to Jeanette. She would often see her paternal grandparents reading it, and would walk away disgusted by their desire to read it. It had never made any sense to her until now.

She was learning and growing in her faith. She didn't at all feel a new sense of purpose or drastic change within herself, though. The reality of her search was not magical as some would think. The weekend after accepting Jesus Christ as her Lord and Savior, she and Anna went to Las Vegas to celebrate Annas twenty-first birthday. Lacking maturity with tainted intentions was how she began her search for God.

Her ill will intentions drove her to learn more about the Bible so she could have debates with her grandpa. It was a twisted way to look at things, and yet, that is where she was in her new found faith and walk with God. And yet, every day brought forth a clearer understanding of who God is. She was recognizing that she had had a warped image of God; always stern with expectation of rules to be obeyed.

She viewed husbands the same way as well. She saw the hate in her grandma's heart for the obligation to stay with her husband who mistreated her before he found the love of God. Because of this experience, by the age of ten, Jeanette had vowed that she would never allow herself to be under submission of a man. The thought of being forced to iron his clothes and cook for him was out of the question for this girl. That protective mindset didn't just seep into her young adulthood years, it grew into a more passionate way of living as she sought answers to life's purpose.

The word "submission" triggered many challenging conversations between her and Michelle. She viewed submission as her enemy and she would do whatever it took to never be under someone's control. She never again wanted to give away her control to someone else to abuse it. She was determined to keep herself protected from such harm. She was adamant that she would never repeat the abuse she endured while trying to love Darryl.

2004 brought a war for Jeanette's heart. She was finding it very difficult to follow God with all the do's and don'ts. She didn't know how to change her behavior, no matter how much she tried. Her only solution was to go on strike from dating in hopes she would eliminate the distractions and draw closer to God.

One day in conversation about her refusal to allow herself to love again and get distracted, her friend from high school, Aaron, made a statement that she had never considered. "You're going to end up marrying Darryl one day," he said matter of factly. Shocked and disturbed at his statement, she immediately dismissed it for she had not even considered that as a possibility.

"Even if he was the last person on earth, we can't ever be together!" her rebuttal sprung forth. Marrying Darryl was not an option and if it were, she hadn't even thought of him as the one she would end up with anymore. That door was closed. She continued her conversation with her friend without bringing Darryl back up again. He was not part of the happily ever after story she was anticipating to have one day.

With the obsession to avoid doing the don'ts, Jeanette was facing temptations difficult to resist. She wanted to love and please God, but each passing day was holding more temptations she didn't feel strong enough to resist. Zaqry was three when she found herself lonely and back in the arms of a young man she had dated while working at the hotel.

She had left this young man the year prior. Although she had enjoyed his attention and admiration, they wanted different things out of life. He was 21 and 2 years older than Jeanette when they dated. Although she found him to be mature, she knew she needed a future of security for her little family. He lived with his parents and spent most of his money on weed, tattoos, alcohol and partying. Although that too is what she originally wanted, and greatly enjoyed partying, she'd wake up the next day with regrets. Regrets that she was selling herself short. These regretful thoughts would cross her mind often when she was with him.

It wasn't always roses and butterflies together either. They would also get into arguments. He was passive though. He didn't engage and feed her monster. He starved it and refused to entertain Jeanette's destructive behavior. At first, Jeanette appreciated someone who didn't rise up against her. Soon enough, those feelings of appreciation faded and she felt ignored. And although they had fun together in this pretend family unit with her son, she knew deep in her heart they didn't have what it would require to keep them magnetized to each other. She desperately wanted things to work out and would compromise only to deceive herself for the inevitable.

One incident that drove a wedge between them was during a "family" weekend vacation to San Diego. Jeanette fought against submission. An argument about how Jeanette was parenting Zaqry led them to derail their hopes to be a family. Zaqry was attempting to get Jeanette's attention, but due to Jeanette's lack of parental skills, she just saw Zaqry throwing a fit. She was doing her hair so she could take her toddler downstairs for breakfast, but it was taking longer than Zaqry understood, plus his growling belly was causing him to be less patient and unwilling to cooperate.

Zaqry was so hungry and angry (hangry) that he pushed the screen door out of its secure location. It flung from their hotel balcony and onto the balcony of the guests one floor down. Freaking out in fear that Zaqry could potentially fall from the balcony, Jeanette yelled at her son. Embarrassed and thankful for the guests one floor below them, she thanked them for giving back the screen door. Her embarrassment led her to deflect and avoid confrontation with the young man willing to take on this role of fatherhood. Instead of embracing his concern and care for her and Zaqry, she pushed him away in hopes he'd understand her brokenness.

Although Jeanette knew nothing about parenting, she was not about to let this guy tell her how to raise her son. "Zaqry is not his son," she justified in her mind. And yet, she desperately wanted a father figure for Zaqry. Jeanette dismissed his response about wanting to be Zaqry's dad. She was surprised at how uneasy his desire made her feel.

Surely, this is what life looks like now for a single teen mom. She found a guy willing to be with her and her son and yet here she is rejecting him and the idea that they could raise Zaqry together. She was deceived into believing she was the final authority over Zaqry's upbringing. She didn't truly take into account this young man standing in front of her to be part of her little family.

The three hour traffic-filled drive home went by in silence, as Jeanette stared out the window with thoughts playing tug-of-war with her heart. Confusion encircled Jeanette's mind as her heart ached at the direction their relationship was headed. Not that it could not be salvaged, but Jeanette had an inability to walk in humility. She was too proud to admit her part in the mess they found themselves in. It was easier to avoid and blame others for not being what she wanted instead of facing the scary parts within herself. They precariously continued their relationship with uncertainties to what the future held for them.

Moments of hope would at times fill Jeanette's heart though. There were times where they seemed to be doing great. This young man was trustworthy and dependable. Her heart wanted things to work out. When she needed someone to watch Zaqry for small periods of time, so she could go to work, Jeanette would call him and he was there. He was reliable. Would she really end things because of the nagging happening deep down in her heart? The debate went on in Jeanette's mind and heart until she was faced with an alarming situation.

The incident that "woke" her up from the glamorized delusion of her happily-ever-after happening came like the pain and sting of a cold shower. They sat at a parking lot at one of their destinations for a "family" outing. This young man, who was good to her, foolishly or purposely severed their relationship beyond repair. He had the audacity to light his pipe and smoke weed in the car with Jeanette's toddler son in the car. Jeanette was shocked at what she had just witnessed. He had never done that before. She was angry, but more so at herself for being so taken by this guy that she was subjecting her son to a second degree high. She quickly took Zaqry out of the car and silently made her point.

Shortly after that day, they ended their relationship with the help of Jeanette's 2 classmates from college who were at one point single teen moms themselves. These friends had asked more questions than offered advice. They allowed Jeanette to speak and hear herself justify things. Jeanette needed to come to her decision and not be swayed one way or another. Afterall, she was the only one that would live with the consequences to her decision. They felt for her and her predicament. Their wisdom showed it. Jeanette felt their compassion and support with whatever decision she made.

Jeanette thought of those wisdom-filled ladies as she lay naked in her ex-boyfriend's arms that fall of 2004. She was beaten by loneliness. It won and overpowered her before she even had a fighting chance. She had no intentions to find herself yo-yoed back into his life, but there she was seeking comfort. Her shame was beginning to cripple her and she was distraught and disgusted with herself.

Before he left that morning, she invited him to go to church with her. His confused face made it clear that he couldn't step foot in a church after the night they had just spent together. Although he wasn't close to God, he feared Him and knew better than to show his face after a night where they sinned against Him. His embarrassed laugh of unbelief turned to shock when he realized Jeanette was serious in her invitation. He sheepishly accepted her invitation and told her he'd come by in the morning so they could go together.

Jeanette waited outside that morning. When the appointed time of their meeting came and went, Jeanette didn't give it a second thought and left to church without him. She took that as her sign from God to remove herself from that temptation. She didn't let her curiosity get the best of her and did not entertain the thought of following up to see what happened. She just allowed that moment to be the pivotal piece that made her stronger to resist the once existing urge to be in his arms.

She drove to church that day with her car speakers blasting "White Flag" by Dido. She occasionally prayed for him and hoped he was safe. She never heard from him again.

Chapter 8

THE COURT HEARING THAT CHANGED EVERYTHING

In early 2005, Jeanette received court documents. Darryl was petitioning to decrease the already small amount of child support he paid her. Her new spiritual mom, Michelle, and Jeanette prayed together during their regular bible studies. She didn't know how to pray, but she talked to God about the situation. She asked Him to be with her. They prayed over the court date Jeanette would have with Darryl.

By then Jeanette's faith in God was becoming stronger and stronger. She knew God would be with her and her heart was postured in expectancy for peace and a fair outcome. Darryl too was believing for a favorable outcome–to pay less in child support. Half his paycheck was going to child support and he didn't trust that it was making its way to Zaqry. He didn't want to support Jeanette's lifestyle of dating other guys. With disgust, he could envision Jeanette spending it with her boyfriend.

The night before Darryl headed down to southern California for the court hearing, he found himself on his knees weeping before God. As he cried out, with tears on his face, Darryl vowed, "Lord, I know you *could* give Jeanette and Zaqry back to me and back in my life but I don't know if you *would*. If you do, I will live my life for you from now on." With that spoken and heart-felt vow, Darryl loaded his drugs, money, and clothes for the trip. Whether his prayer had the faith as small as a mustard seed or not, Darryl layed that request and left it at God's throne.

Court was held on Thursday, March 2nd of 2005. Darryl and Jeanette hadn't seen each other for almost a year. They would talk over the phone, but that was the extent to their communication. Darryl and Jeanette were different people than they were the last time they saw each other. Jeanette's journey of faith was becoming more and more apparent. Darryl's ability to tame his monster, Anger, was noticeable. Neither, Jeanette nor Darryl, expected the outcome from that hearing.

Jeanette and her parents sat in the waiting area as Darryl walked in. Jeanette did everything in her power to avoid eye contact. She was not going to show any signs of weakness. Intrigued by his exposed sadness, something began to take place within Jeanette's heart. Her heart began to feel compassion for Darryl.

Lunch break was announced before they were able to see the judge for their case. With a more tenderized heart, Jeanette asked Darryl to join her and her parents for lunch. They went home, sat at the kitchen table and talked. It was the first time in a long time that they had been able to talk without anger triggering their voice to broadcast hate. They were nervously at peace talking with one another that they ran out of time to eat. They headed back to court without any source of nourishment to their hungry bellies.

Their time came and they faced the judge. They stood in avoidance as the judge asked questions. The judge favored Jeanette and did not decrease the child support amount Darryl needed to pay. Strangely enough that was not the last time Jeanette saw Darryl.

Darryl's truck was impounded a few days prior to the court hearing and he was left without transportation to go back home from the hearing. She ended up taking him to his friend's house where he was staying for the duration of his visit.

She pulled up and parked. They sat parked in front of the house talking. They shared of their endured past pain, fears, and love for one another. Their conversation was harmonious without ruffles or snags. "Could this be more than co-parenting?" was the thought that entered their minds. They wanted to dismiss this thought, but it was clear they were not the same immature teenagers they once were. They had time to grow up per se. The time apart showed to be just what they needed to help parent Zaqry together.

Through that impactful conversation that day, Darryl and Jeanette ended up starting a path toward reconciliation. Evidently unknowing what lay ahead, they both somehow felt this peace that supassed all understanding within them.

Gary and Michelle offered for Darryl to live with them to help him be close to Zaqry and be the dad they both knew he could be. Darryl started working at a mall nearby selling shoes. During all his available moments he would make it a point to see Zaqry and Jeanette.

During one day out together, Darryl experienced a weight lift from his shoulders that he hadn't recognized was there. For a while now, Zaqry had been calling Darryl by his first name because Jeanette had forced him to. In the car while on their way to get In-N-Out burgers, Jeanette corrected Zaqry. "You can call him daddy. He's your daddy." Zaqry knew that was his dad this whole time and now he was free to call him what he'd been wishing to call him for as long as he could remember.

A smile beamed from Zaqry's face so brightly. For the first time in a long time, he released the words his heart knew about the man sitting with him. "Daddy, can I have this please?" It was as if every muscle in Darryl's body lost function and he melted at hearing that word come forth from his son's lips. Darryl took in breath differently from that day forward. It was as if cleaner oxygen entered his lungs and he now had the ability to release the weight that no longer needed to be carried. Without saying a word, his gratitude-filled face expressed a powerful "thank you" to Jeanette.

Shocked at what was happening, Jeanette found herself in a new level of confusion she did not expect. This uncertainty brought her to her pen and paper once again. Her journal entry captured her hesitancy and discussion with God. She bracketed what she heard and sensed from God:

I Corinthians 6:18 3/21/05

"Don't be immoral in the matters of sex. That is a sin against your own body in a way that no other sin is. You surely know that your body is a temple where the Holy Spirit lives. The Spirit is in you and is a gift from God. You are no longer your own. God paid a great price for you. So use your body to honor God."

Papa Chuy!
You know my situation. I am at fault. I committed adultery against you. Please forgive me. Restore me, Lord. Make me PURE. Thank you, Lord. I'm sorry for falling into temptation. Please give me strength to push our enemy away when I am tempted again. Please let it be Your words I use against him, Lord. The enemy will not win. I will grow and learn from this experience.

Thank You for forgiving my immoral sin. Thank you for the opportunity to be forgiven.

I Corinthians 7:8 3/22/05

"...But those who marry will have a lot of trouble, and I want to protect you from that."

Papa Chuy!

Guide me Daddy! Show me the path I am to take concerning marriage. How is it that before when I saw him I became disgusted, but now all I see is beauty? He has a beautiful soul. He may still have his temper as everyone else has, but his spirit is so joyful :) He's smiling. I'm smiling. We still have our differences to work out and we will have confrontations about things, but Lord, I have faith that everything will be great because you are with us. Marriage sounds very difficult, but with Your love for us and our love for You, we will be okay. More than okay, we will be blessed. [In due time - please be patient]. Thank You. :)

Your forever daughter,

Jeanette

I Corinthians 11:11 3/26/05

"As far as the Lord is concerned, men and women need each other."

Papa Chuy!

Thank You for giving Darryl to me; for bringing him to me and vice versa, Lord. Give me knowledge Lord. Give me the mind I need to make proper decisions concerning marrying Darryl. You showed me something today while listening to K-Wave. We must be a match in soul, spirit, and I think heart/mind -not sure which one it was but in any case, I'll need four matches. In time with the faith I have in You (we have in You) things will be just fine. We will rest ourselves unto You. Thank you for the opportunity I now have by you sending him to me.

Your forever daughter,
Jeanette

Through their new-found unexpected peace and calm interactions with one another. They felt strongly that marriage was the next step in their relationship. During their three months of wedding planning to prepare for marriage, they entertained the thought of eloping. They both desired their marriage to not be just a signed county document, but they saw their union as a marriage covenant. They desired to enter into a marriage covenant vowing their whole lives to God and to each other. They planned to get matching covenant mark tattoos of 3 interlocked rings on their forearms as a reminder that their marriage could only be sustained through both being interlocked with God and each other.

Planning their wedding had become emotionally taxing on them both. Each side of the family had their opinions of who should and should not attend the wedding. To try to figure this out was leading both Darryl and Jeanette into a new path. They decided no one was allowed to attend. They were not going to allow anyone to ruin their special day. Gary, Darryl's previous foster dad and Michelle's husband, married them in a private ceremony; they eloped.

No one showed up that day as expected. The music was cued. Zaqry began to walk Jeanette down the aisle as her bare feet were now treading the way for a new role she would soon possess. She was going to be Darryl's wife. That moment was surreal. To think she'd ever marry Darryl had at one point been impossible to imagine and yet there she was holding his hands.

Darryl's (foster) brother, Myles, took photos and captured their reunited union. Eli, Darryl's younger (foster) brother, displayed great maturity that day as he looked after Zaqry. That morning Crystal Cove in NewPort Beach, CA looked differently. It held hope for their future. The wedding was simple yet significant.

Immediately following their marriage vows, both Darryl and Jeanette got baptized by Michelle. In planning their big day, Jeanette felt stirred to once again change her name. She was intrigued by Saul's story along with others whom God changed their names during either their conversion or a significant moment in their lives. Going by a new name brought a revelation to those in the Bible that they are not who they once were. Jeanette decided to begin going by Lluvi, pronounced "you-vee," after coming up from the icy water in the Corona Del Mar cove.

After their baptism, together they enjoyed a meal at Mimi's Cafe with great smiles and yet a slither of apprehensiveness as to how their story would unfold. They lacked the resources to have a honeymoon, so they went home to their new apartment while Gary and Michlle kept Zaqry overnight. They ventured out for a hike in Palm Springs the next day and began their journey of life together.

Maybe marriage was the right thing; maybe not. They couldn't tell at that point. They just knew they loved each other and wanted to be with one another. "Maybe their little family could be salvaged," they thought. Hope sparked in both their hearts. Lluvi was drawn to Darryl like magnets powerfully attach to one another.

Their passion to rebuild the brokenness was clear to both of them. They were ready to put in the work required. They understood, they were faced with heavy baggage they carried into their marriage. Gary directly and boldly broke it down to them that if they didn't take care of the damage made, the weight of the baggage they are bringing into the marriage would weigh them down and soon lead to an even greater devastated separation.

The divorce rate within Christians who attend

church regularly is similar to those who don't attend church. Knowing and walking with God doesn't seem to have a great determining factor to the success of a marriage. As confusing as that may be, Darryl and Lluvi learned quickly that although they love each other, the love for themselves would at times supersede their love for one another. Even coming together and establishing boundaries was not the protective force that could bind them from tugs this world had to offer. Still, they tried all they knew to do.

They established the definition of infidelity. Their previous relationship with one another was full of confusion because they each seemed to have been speaking two different languages. This time, Lluvi wanted to walk in clarity. "Why were words so tricky," she thought as she reflected on those past memories.

To Darryl and Lluvi, infidelity means allowing someone else to fulfill only what the husband and wife are to satisfy. They were determined that no one else could play their part. They established this by starting with their emotions. They committed that day that people outside their marriage no longer had the permission to lead them astray through their kindness and friendliness.

People will be kind and friendly, they can't control others, but they can control themselves.They can stay active and be keen to their own emotions to get a better reading and understanding of the path that their emotions would lead them. If they each at all felt like a person outside their marriage was fulfilling an emotional desire that only Darryl or Lluvi were allowed to fulfill, then they must walk away. This included existing and future friendships. The friends of opposite sex that they each had could not enter into that established level of closeness with them any longer.

Although the definition of infidelity was established, the first year into their marriage was more than Lluvi expected. Lluvi wanted out just as quickly as they said "I do". Although they had beautiful peaceful moments of harmony, they didn't realize they were constantly being triggered into the pain from the past. Little did they know that they were each other's trigger. Lluvi would catch Darryl in lies and devastation would choke her yet again.

Reality hit. She remembered the pain of his deception. He was not honest about small and insignificant things. They were unnecessary lies. These lies were sprinkled all over these truths and half truths for whatever reason. Lluvi found herself again not being able to trust Darryl. She questioned every word making it impossible for him to please her. She became angry at his deception. She no longer just accused him, she once again began to attack him. She was tired of being the one feeling the blows by his lies. She wanted out. She was done. It was exhausting to be on high alert all the time without any respite from her thoughts.

Their relationship came to a head one night. The

anguish was eating at Lluvi. She turned on the bedroom light to read the Bible and journal in hopes it would calm her down. With the evening being late and Darryl needing to sleep, he turned off the light. They went back and forth turning on and off the bedroom light, until bam! They didn't. As soon as Darryl turned off the light for the last time, Lluvi curled her fingers into her fist and punched him in the face. He was not expecting to physically fight. Instinctively, he restrained her with all his body weight. They were both in shock at what just happened. How could people who claim to love God physically hurt one another? They both thought.

The yelling and screaming was what their son heard muffled through the walls of his bedroom. Pulling the covers over his head, he sang himself to sleep. Zaqry heard more anger than joy in his home. At four, he didn't understand how they couldn't be happy. He couldn't understand why his mom cried as much as she did. He didn't understand why he would find her weeping and praying in her closet. Zaqry loved his dad, "why can't mommy love him too?" he'd question silently. Why was his mom not having fun like he was when dad was around? Similar confusing thoughts went through this little human mind as he tried to understand his world and everyone in it.

Darryl was about to call the police and send Lluvi to jail for domestic violence, but something stopped him. Whether it was the compassion he felt for his son, or memories of his parents handcuffed, he's not sure, but he felt a halt in his desire to call the police. He ended up calling Gary and Michelle. It was late. They had their family in bed and yet they found a way and made it to their rescue.

As they sat across from them in their tiny little apartment, they spoke truth in love to them. They couldn't address every detail to the behavior that had them in this place, but they addressed the big boulder like rocks that kept weighing them down. They couldn't be the ones to fix their marriage; only Darryl and Lluvi had the power and ability to do so. A physical trainer can guide, model, instruct and correct the athlete's form and exercise, but cannot do the work for him or her. Similarly, Gary and Michelle could not do the work for Darryl and Lluvi.

That sounded exhausting for Lluvi. She was out of adrenaline for this fear-filled marriage. Her endurance level had dropped severely. She was spent by having to be alert to every word Darryl spoke. There was no rest and yet "the only way to succeed is to overcome this?" her mind battled. Unsure she could continue, Lluvi stayed quiet. Her heart was hiding her away in her dark mansion once more. The feeling of being trapped swallowed her alive once again.

Darryl too felt trapped; trapped by all the parameters Lluvi set up so she could keep tabs on him. She was attempting to control everything and it was driving him insane. He felt like those caged animals in research facilities. Researchers gawking and taking notes. Lluvi was not just looking for admiration sake, she was looking intently to find his imperfections. "Lluvi is intentionally looking to find my weak spots," he thought to himself. He felt she was no longer his support but instead his opposition. He was in fact right. Lluvi was not for him. She was for herself which consequently positioned herself against him.

No matter what they heard from their pastor and read in the Bible about the truth; they still saw each other as enemies. They knew the scripture in Ephesians that teaches them that they "don't wrestle against flesh and blood, but against principalities, against powers, against the rulers of the darkness of this world, against spiritual hosts of wickedness in heavenly places" and yet, what they saw, heard, and felt was that they were in fact each other's enemy. They were both in survival mode giving to each other what they could. The problem they didn't understand nor recognize was that they were in fact trying to survive from a place of lack.

They didn't know how to love one another. Their lives taught them to take care of themselves and look out for number one. They found themselves living out The Allegory of the Long Spoons. This powerful parable, attributed to Rabbi Haim of Romshisok, shows the difference between people in heaven and hell. Both parties are forced to eat with long spoons. "In each location, the inhabitants are given access to food, but the utensils are too unwieldy to serve oneself with." In hell, guests only try to feed themselves and can't because the spoons are too long. The people there cannot cooperate, and consequently starve. In heaven, the diners feed one another across the table and thrive. Love and unity abides in heaven.

Both Darryl and Lluvi had what it took to care for one another, but they were consumed by only taking care of themselves. Their fear that they were the only ones who could care for themselves was a lie that trapped them. They went to marriage workshops and maintained their ongoing weekly dinners with Gary and Michelle with some success. They had moments of peace, but they were not lasting moments. Those moments of peace were always followed by moments of misery.

Chapter 9

INTENTIONAL TO COVER

As life continued with its uncertainties, Darryl's tendencies to lie and cover up would arise again. When it did, after instinctively attacking Darryl, Lluvi would hide in her closet to hide her tears from him. That closet began to be the new home to her secret place with God. She began to cover Darryl in prayer through her anguish cries of heartache. She used 2 Corinthians 5:17, "Therefore, if anyone is in Christ, he is a new creation; old things have passed away; behold, all things have become new." She took hold of that truth and began to call forth Darryl as a new creation in Christ which meant that old things had passed away.

As Lluvi mumbled, then uttered, and shouted forth this truth in tears, she began to behold that all things have become new. In her closet she'd hide in tears to call forth this truth. Maybe it was psyching herself out. Or maybe she was able to enter into a new understanding of the spiritual realm. For days she spoke this out. Days turned to weeks and weeks turned to months. There were some hints that Darryl's heart was being impacted by her prayers, but not enough to relent and stop proclaiming this truth in the secret place with God.

In the natural, Darryl's behavior was of old, not this new creation God talked about in His word, and yet Lluvi could now see beyond the natural. Lluvi was relentless to see what she caught in the spirit take place in the natural. She understood that humans had been given free will, so it was not a wish upon the star type of prayer that magically would turn Darryl into her dream pictured husband. No, the reality was still that Darryl held free will and could be and do anything he wanted to. There were moments where she lost hope and he would deceive her and she'd find herself wishing upon her death so that the torment would stop.

Again, she captured her raw and real emotions in the comfort of her letters to God.

1/12/06

Oh, the thoughts that run through my mind. How I would love to stop worrying. Daddy, I don't know what I'm doing. The world seems to be pulling us apart.

Darryl's so consumed in the world and loves it. I've

figured out why I liked being up North with his friends. The world didn't seem to possess them. Down here Darryl and I barely talk; he's either watching TV or playing video games on the computer and I'm either reading or writing. We used to read together. We used to write to each other back and forth, but that died. He wrote nothing deep. I don't see this relationship growing stronger, but deteriorating at a steady pace.

I'm tired Daddy. I feel dragged down. I don't think this is what I'm supposed to be about. I have the most ugliest thoughts. I sometimes want to just run. I want to go home! Then I think how stupid I am for wanting to drive into something and die. I have a son to take care of-the son You gave me The son I promised to love forever. The son that holds the key to my heart. The son I don't spend enough time with anymore. The son that runs to his room when his feelings are hurt. The son who loves me no matter what. The son who needs me to be there. The son that I must protect. I must protect him from my word's destruction.

I need to start with our home. I don't want him listening to all the yelling and arguing. He will NOT grow up thinking it's okay and acceptable. Darryl and I have already ruined the foundation to this relationship we call a "marriage."

This marriage is full of abuse; both physical and verbal. Daddy, I HATE the thoughts I have; I know better, but I still wish and hope horrible things. And Darryl being jobless makes it more difficult. He doesn't seem to look for a job. I'm not quite sure where he's at or what he's doing, but I know he's not looking. I hate feeling like his mother. I'm always on his butt, making sure he did what he's supposed to.

I always want to sleep and get away from all this. My dreams show me things. The feelings I have in my dreams are happy, sometimes I'm scared, but never for very long. In my dreams You're there. You show me things I don't see or hear with all the distractions of the world.

Daddy, I want out! I don't think I'm supposed to be where I am in life. I think I'm being held back from what I'm supposed to, but I don't really know what that is either.

I feel like I'm in a submarine and Darryl is always opening the door and letting in water. I close the door, but later he does the same thing. The more he does it the more water comes in and I panic. I'm tired Daddy. I'm tired of worrying and as often as I give You my burdens the more I end up having because the door is open and water runs in.

The life I was reaching for has nothing Darryl's life consists of. I want to go to church every week and know You more. I want to talk to You with him daily. I want to read Your word daily. I want to write to You daily. I want...I want to be happy.

Darryl just took a pillow and blanket to sleep in the living room. Daddy, this marriage is done. I don't know what else to do. I don't know if I even wanna do anything about this anymore. Alex is going over to my mom's to get his brakes fixed by my uncle. There's something about him that just doesn't seem right. I told Darryl to leave yesterday. I'm tired of having to deal with everything.

Daddy, 1/31/06

End of the month is here and as stressful as it was, I made a point to forget it all when I got home. I made dinner for us. I went to my mom's for some eggs (we're out). I made pancakes, egg omelets w/broccoli, potatoes and sausages and yet I was unappreciated.

I wanted to hurry and wash his dishes; the ones he didn't wash last night because of a movie. He wanted to watch another movie tonight and promised to wash them tonight, but Daddy he said that last night. Daddy, I'm picking up after him and taking care of him and it doesn't seem enough. There's always something else.

He ordered me to make Zaqry's lunch for tomorrow. Daddy, I've been making our lunches this week, but the way he treats me is so awful. It's like no matter what I do, it's just never enough.

He seems distracted and never paying attention. He says he doesn't want to rent a house anymore; that he's not ready. Daddy, I'm here no matter what. I know that if we're to rent a house You'll show us what we need to do. It feels like he's deliberately trying to hurt me. Not less than an hour ago he was saying that he'll go in early one day and will go to Huntington Beach to the home rental place and now he says he's not ready. What?

I don't get him. I just have to sit back, vent to You and let You tell me what I need to know. He's been through so much, Daddy. He's come from a completely different life than what You've given me. I know that he's never actually had a truly loving family and I make it so difficult for him to love me.

He says I need to stop treating him like a little kid and that I'm not his mother. Daddy, sometimes I feel like it. I know that he needs a mother's love not a mother's discipline. Daddy, that's where You come in. You're to guide him through life. You are molding him to what You want him to be. Thank You for holding us in Your hands. I love you.

Daddy, 2/10/06

I feel Your presence; I feel You with me; I feel Your strength; I feel Your protection. Nothing makes sense to me [nothing's supposed to make sense; My way is not man's way].

Daddy, I feel lost, I'm turning around in circles to find out which direction to go...I see the path I am to take and it's pointing to Arizona. Daddy, I don't want to hesitate, but I'm scared.

[Why are you scared if I'm holding you; I've got you in

My hands, you are My child. You mean too much to Me to let you slip away. You will be moving from one place to another...I don't want you tied down. You must know that I command all. The trees will not grow without Me; the wind will not be, the sun will not shine. I have spoken. You're distracting yourself-you make things harder for yourself-let go...go...listen...go...

All that you have, I bring you. All the things you've gone through, I have allowed-it makes you who I want you to be. You will go through pain...lots of it, but you will not be broken-you will not break, but only if you believe. You've got to trust Me. I've got you. If I ask you to walk (on water towards Me, will you get scared and start to drown? Believe all that I can do. Believe and let go. I can't pull you in to me completely if you're still holding on to the old.]

Later that day Lluvi writes again to God….

Darryl left me again. He always leaves when my questions get the best of me. He thinks it's some sort of game to dangle me from a string. He knows I'm at my weakest and seems to love it. He's supposed to be here no matter what. He's hardly ever here-his mind's always elsewhere. I never have his full attention. He gets mad at me when I cry.

Everytime this happens, Daddy, I just want to go home. I don't want to do this anymore. I hate feeling so unloved. I feel like I mean nothing to him. He's always gone when I need him the most. He came back in to criticize me and make me feel even worse. It's bad enough I hate myself. I don't need him doing so too.

3/17/06

Do not condemn yourself to the world. I know he's not there yet and neither are you. Don't take the steps back because you will lose your way forward. The steps you've taken in the past have disappeared. How can you step back without falling?

You are My child and I love you. Who else needs to love you for you to love yourself but Me? Why can't you see what I see? You are beautiful to Me! Listen to Me with your heart-don't believe what the world has to say.

The enemy will do everything it can to create the division between you two. Be careful Lluvi, he will try to get you, but you need to know the Truth. I am Truth. I am the Way. I am Life. Pay attention; he will get him if he can. If he can't, he will try through you. Don't hold his anger against him; he does not know what he's doing.

Your pain is different from his. Your pain is the same as his. You must help him before he is strong enough to help you. Just because you're weak at that moment does not mean I am not working on your healing process.

Help him Lluvi. Help My child. He's crying in a whole

different way than you do. Do not ignore it or pretend it doesn't exist. He will not want you near at first, but he just needs to know you'll try again to show that you haven't given up on him.

Wipe his tears, they come out through the anger in his voice. Be careful of the words you put out there; comfort him. He' in pain Lluvi. Don't worry, I've got you in My hands, just don't step back because you will fall. Keep your eyes on Me and know that I've got you. Have faith, Lluvi; it will get better but before it does wounds must heal. Healing does not happen overnight. I must clean all that's been infected-it will sting; you will shed tears, but look at Me.

I will show you the end results, just stay focused. Keep your eyes set on Me. Don't look at your surroundings; you will stumble. Keep your eyes on Me and you will get through this; just keep your eyes on Me. I've got you! I love you My dearest child.

-Daddy

Lluvi found comfort in the love letters from God. The situation was still swinging on highs and lows, but she was hopeful in the direction to walk. She was determined to love Darryl in spite of his behavior and words. Divorce still lured her to give up and let him be, but through her conversations with God, she regained perspective and strength to continue. It was not easy and she continued to face the relationship's hardships, yet God's words rang in her ear and her heart would regain strength to endure the inevitable pain.

During yet another moment of Darryl's deceptive survival mechanism, Lluvi found herself staring in the mirror in her room in silence. She was in search of a release to the agony she was experiencing. She knew Darryl loved her and yet she felt so unloved. Why was Darryl continuing to disregard her feelings? Memories from her pregnancy filled her mind like the times before. She felt her blood rise to the surface of her skin. She felt heat emit from her pores. This rejection was heavier than she could bear. She could not find the answers she needed.

Moments prior, Darryl was encircling her with his words, causing her to feel crazy. His gaslighting was unrecognizable so there she went in circles with Darryl's words. Unknowingly, she would take the bait and his deception would fling her around like a fish out of water as she tried to regain control and find oxygen.

Darryl was furious that she continued to ask the same question in many different forms. "Why can't she just trust me!?" he baffled silently. He was lost as to how one simple slip up of his words could cause her venomous monster to coil in preparation of an attack. He knew she listened and watched him closely when it came to any other females. He couldn't share fully of his day because of fear that jealousy would arise and explode forth from Lluvi. It wasn't his fault girls found him attractive. He wasn't doing anything wrong, he thought. "I'm just friendly, " he reasoned.

Frustratedly, his mind went in search to find blame in Lluvi. "Friendly is a great attribute to have, what's wrong with Lluvi!" "Oh God, Lluvi, don't start." pierced his passive aggressive remark right into her rejected heart. "What's wrong with you?" he barked in her face. "You always have to find something to argue about," he continued. "We were fine and now you had to start. When will my answers be good enough for you?!" he abrasively emphasized.

His words felt like sharp slaps to Lluvi's face. She was oblivious to his feelings at this point. Her main concern was obtaining the truth of his whereabouts. It shot her back to her last trimester of pregnancy where she found a blanket in the trunk of Darryl's car. Curiously, she asked whose it was. With a well composed matter of fact expression, he responded and said, "it's my friend, Erin's." Darryl ensured he had a long yet short enough pause before starting his next sentence. "You remember Aaron, don't you? We used to play football together."

Now, as the reader, you can clearly see the different spelling to the names Erin and Aaron. Unfortunately, both sound exactly the same, but also unfortunately for Lluvi, Erin is the female version of that name. With little awareness of this deceptive strategy, she was easily fooled yet again.

Darryl had many moments where his crafty tongue got the best of her. But now, she was no longer a 17 year old emotionally pregnant girl. She was 21 and aware of the devious way Darryl articulated his answers. She understood his intentional responses to buy himself time as he crafted and formulated his answers. She was done being fooled and deceived. Unfortunately, that is the beauty of deception; one is unaware he or she is being deceived. Feelings of insanity ensnared Lluvi from being able to think clearly.

The room began to spin as Darryl and Lluvi wrestled around with their words slashing each other as swordsmen attack to protect themselves. Each laceration was now penetrating greater pain to their already wounded hearts. A heavy level of weariness overtook their battle. Again, they each left wounded and defeated only to reconvene this match again another day when more ammo was refueled within them.

And so was their life as husband and wife. In circles they "played" this game of secrecy. Neither had the courage to expose their true feelings. Neither had the bravery to enter into the unknown world of transparency. They each locked themselves away from each other for fear that transparency would give the other powerful ammo to cause irreparable and severe damage to their hearts.

This game cycled in and out as waves do when they crash onto the shoreline. It was patterned. Each of them could only take so much BS "bologna sandwiches" from one another. Each feared to address anything in fear that war would break out and yet, the more bottling up that took place, the more was accumulating for when the explosion would take place. So much shaking was taking place to those bottled up emotions that like clockwork, one would explode causing a ripple effect. As soon as one exploded, it would induce the other one's emotional bottle to detonate.

The explosions caused such a great mess, and no one wanted to clean up that filth. After days of giving each other the silent treatment, the filth was somehow swept and covered up with a rug to protect those precious memories from spreading. The rug was continuing to be a hazard as they both tripped over the heap that formed in trying to conceal the filth their words produced. Within time, they both somehow relocated the heap into a large closet where they would close the door in hopes that out of sight meant out of mind.

Chapter 10

RETURN OF THE DARK CASTLE

Lluvi loved her son more than anything so ending her life was a thought she would push out as soon as it tried to invade her dark castle. No, this time darkness would not overpower her. She would not reattempt to end things for good. This time Lluvi was facing internal monsters that berated her thoughts.

She loved God. She knew He had a great plan for her life. She knew God loved her greatly and that she was His beloved. She knew all this and more, yet she was not strong enough to battle her thoughts of divorce. The anxiety level would come in waves. Her relationship with Darryl felt as if she was on a never ending roller coaster. It would take her up and down. It swerved and jolted her in such abrasive manners. She felt as if she was constantly taken by surprise through this roller coaster of emotions that at times felt she was upside down and right side up again all in one day.

This time Lluvi did not need her stomach pumped from overdosing or forced to drink the nasty black drink to remove poison from her body. No, this time, with every ounce of strength she refrained from cutting her skin with a blade. Although she was strengthened to not engage in those destructive behaviors, she was not strong enough by this overpowering sensation to brutally scratch her arms.

Her sharp nails were just as vicious as a dull knife. Her nails were mild enough to not cause a deathly tragedy. This impulse would overtake her as she hid in her closet in tears of the torment she felt. This cycle of dysfunction within their marriage generated the feeling of being trapped. Seeing no way out in those waves of dark times, she could not see hope. Her fierce fingernails were a tool to help release the bottled up pain within her. In agony filled-tears, Lluvi screamed in her pillow while blood flowed from her skin.

Bringing her raw emotions onto paper, she again cried out to God in her letters. These letters helped bring her right side up again. The letters she wrote in her journal allowed all those mixed and tangled emotions to arise. It was her security blanket through the scary storms she'd regularly face. It brought comfort and eased the pain like pain medication does. The pain is still there, but the body no longer responds to it as it's masked by the medication.

All letters to God were not always during her moments of pain though. She loved God and desired to know Him more and more. Not just like a superhero saving her from the dangers in her life, but as her Father God, who loved her no matter what. He was not her firefighter only coming onto the scene because her home was on fire, No, Lluvi wanted more than the surface-type of relationship with God; she wanted to grow in her love for Him more and more each day. Her journal entries again, capture her unprocessed emotions and thoughts of this young 22 year old mind and heart.

Daddy, 4/8/06

I hate that I only write to You during ugly times. It seems as if I only need You during bad times when in fact I need You ALL the time; during good and bad. I want to praise You during good and thank You during bad.

Today was awesome, Daddy! I was scared to go to Abby's baby shower because I was afraid of the past. I didn't want more memories about my pregnancy coming back.

It's too much for me Daddy. I lie! You know what I can bear. You know what's too much for me. You won't give me anything I can't handle and I love You for that. Sometimes it seems to me that I can't handle it, but I don't understand Your will or plans for my life. You have me in Your hands. The only way to go wrong is to leave You.

Ephesians 4:1-3 6/7/06

You have shown me what path to take right now, but I haven't yet. Daddy, how do I do that, he won't let me [just love him. Just love him and he will unlock the door to his heart and I will break down the barrier he has created] I must love the unlovable. I love You

Ephesians 4:15: to speak the truth in LOVE; show me how Daddy, speak it for me until I get it.

Ephesians 4:18,20,26,28-29:

Daddy, he stole my heart when I was being fooled by his love for You. He must not steal again, but work for it. How do I love someone that must work for my heart/love? [limits] Give little?

[No, give all holding back nothing, little by little give him what you've got of the truth, give him affection and compliments even when he's undeserving, show him that no matter what, you're still there pouring out your love for him just as I did for all My children]

If he rejects me? [Then proceed with more love, you will see a difference in his response, give time, give effort, give what you've got, he will one day receive it. I love you, be strong and know I am God.] I love You, Daddy. I will start on my mission. I love You.

Forever your daughter
~*Lluvi*~

My Lluvi 7/6/06

[Pick up little by little. I will only give you what you can handle. I will carry you through the rough patches and lead you toward healing. I am and will be here for you.

Do not be afraid. You can do all things through Christ who strengthens you. I will give you peace when you ask. I will be here no matter what.] Thank you Daddy

Lluvi knew that love kept no record of wrongs. Her writings were her way of securing her sanity. Recording this night's events in letter form to God was her way of feeling less crazy. This time she was keeping a time log of her pain and how God met her in the very midst of her despair.

10/1/06 11:30pm

"Nasty pig b*tch!" says Darryl with a voice full of disgust. "Why does he care anyway?" I wonder. He doesn't seem to care as I try to cry myself to sleep. But to pound on both bathroom doors loud enough to wake our neighbors he'll do, but come to my rescue to try to win this battle he won't. This is by far the hardest battle I have had to fight.

All my life I have fought and fought, but to this day I am nowhere closer to winning. With eyes full of judgment, I see him looking at me. With eyes that don't understand. With eyes that do not see me; that don't want to see me. He does not want to know me; the me that runs scared every time something new comes along. The me that cannot understand my ways. The me that hurts inside when I feel all alone. The me that needs more than a partner, who belongs to the world and its ways, but I need a best friend who does not ask why I'm in trouble, but asks how he can help to free me from it.

He's asked me why I hurt him with the cruel words that I know will penetrate his mind. I did not answer the question. If he only knew why I did it, he could help me stop! Or worse, he'll know the way of bringing the monster inside me out.

This is a never ending cycle of angry words damaging each other's hearts & soul. The time spent doing so is irreplaceable and cannot be brought back. It is time that cannot forever be changed. At times like these, when I'm at my lowest I wonder what life would have been like if I wouldn't have married him and stop dead in my tracks- <because I cannot see myself anywhere else.> My mind cannot foresee such a time and place.

I do wonder what it will be like when he's had enough of my unexplainable nonsens and leaves. I can't see myself letting go. At times, I say I want him out of my life, but in reality I want the Darryl he's being to get out and leave the Darryl that I have created. My creation will always stay as a mere imagination. Such a person is far from existing - in this world at least.

Writing this, I've realized that I've left the world to find me and be the me I believe I should be. This whole time I've been wanting it to be about me, me, me. I am not here for me! I am here for the soul that is unloved and unappreciated by the ones that are supposed to be here to love him. I am here to make up for all those birthdays without presents. All these days and nights surrounded by people but still felt alone. I am here to help heal the past and prepare for a future.

I cannot go to him now, as I know what type of words will come from his mouth. I just finished saying it was about him, but I'm still afraid for myself.

"Stupid b*tch" he says as he walks towards the living room at 12:15am. "Stupid b*tch, all you want to do is cause an argument" I hear him say as I hear something in the living room fall and break. Daddy, I have no idea what I did? I scooted towards him so he would hold me and carefully moved his arm under me and he started yelling at me; telling me, "it doesn't bend that way."

"Can you position yourself so you can hold me?" I asked a few times as he ignores me. Then after the third time he yells some more telling me, "that's all you had to say".

He stands up. I asked why he was yelling at me, I didn't do anything to him and he starts yelling some more, "that's all you had to say" I beg him to stop yelling at me.

After a couple times, I tell him to just go then and I threw his pillow in the hallway. He's furious now and he grabs his pillow and pushes me to scoot over and I tell him, "You're mad. You can go sleep alone now."

He's hurting me by now with his strength while pushing me towards my side of the bed.
I throw his pillow again so he can leave and he picks it up with two hands and with such hate he hits me on the head with it and leaves calling me that name he uses so freely. He came in fifteen minutes later after hearing me sob to apologize for "overreacting."

This is so hard to intake Daddy. I don't know what I did for him to yell at me so. I just wanted him to hold me. He asks "why? Why? Why?" I don't remember the question. Why can't I remember the question? He wouldn't leave the bedroom until I answered it.

He always says, "If you can't answer it just tell me." He makes me feel so stupid when I can't answer his questions, like I can't comprehend the question in order to answer it. Daddy I don't understand, I don't know what I did to make him yell at me. I know that throwing his pillow didn't make it any better, it made it worse, but I didn't know what to do and I couldn't sleep with him the way he was being.

Before he left, he demanded to know why I have the light on. It's 12:45 am and he just went to bed. I didn't say anything and just went to sleep. I don't understand his actions or thoughts. He reaches to hold me as I pull away to blow my nose and wipe my eyes. He's ready to talk now. But I'm not and I'm sure he'll have some kind of comment for it.

"Why couldn't you just say you wanted me to hold you? Can you answer me? Why didn't you?" Daddy, how was I to know to ask that? I didn't want to wake him up at first so I was being careful in just slowly moving his arm. He's justifying his actions by what I did. What did I do? Trying not to wake him up deserves yelling and a hit in the face (with the pillow) while being called horrible names?

"Please tell me what's going on Lluvi?" He tries to hold me again, but I can't be comforted by someone who less than a minute ago yelled with such disgust. There have been other nights that he's not wanted to hold me.

"It's one o'clock in the morning, how can you have nothing to say, I mean, come on," he says. He won't move towards his side. It's one AM now and he leaves while saying (singing sounds) something under his breath.

Daddy I don't know how to be a good mommy to Zaqry when I'm feeling this cruddy. He doesn't want to believe that he's the reason for my headaches. All incidents like this I cry, then bottle it up and don't talk to him about it and pretend they never happened. They keep building up.

I've noticed that every time I worry and cry over these things, I blow my nose from crying and each time I have a bloody runny nose. He was supposed to be my crying shoulder like the song I walked down the aisle to, but it's because of his turned shoulder that I cry. He doesn't comfort me without wanting whatever answer to his questions. He can't just hold me and love me while I cry.

Today I walked into a messy home. I asked him what he did all day and what he cleaned and he couldn't answer me. He said he cleaned but wouldn't specify what he cleaned other than dusted the TV. I don't know what he does all day. He said he spent 2-3 hours looking for a job, but nothing supports his answers. He sent his resume to a few places, but that's it.

I hate the fact that he can't keep a job. Several weeks before a place fires him, he complains about being unhappy there. I hate that he has the opportunity to leave jobs.

He knows how much I dislike the environment of my job and how painful it is to work there because of my headaches, but he keeps telling me I have to go to work because he doesn't have a job. I hate that he finds places for me to apply when he knows I won't be working anymore. I'm afraid to not work, because I know that once he is unemployed again, he's going to force me to work!

I don't want him being forced to take any job either. He has more potential than to work by Anaheim Stadium or working some dead end job bringing half my income.

He talks to Gary and Michelle about not going back to doing loans but his actions and the places he applies say otherwise. He wants to stick to commission based, quota meeting jobs that are unreliable and untrustworthy. He doesn't want to be a "paper pusher" as he calls me.

Hey! I don't want to be a paper pusher either! But that's all I know right now to be. He doesn't want to start at the bottom because that requires him to be someone's b*tch as he calls it. I don't like being bossed around either, but I need to swallow my pride and do what I have to in order to keep a roof over my family's head and food on our table. It's now 1:30am. There's so much pressure for me to be this family's back-bone, but I see myself getting weaker with every blow to my heart.

Recognizing blind spots comes first with the understanding that they exist. Lluvi, in her immature state, was unaware of the dangers these blind spots bring. Blind spots need to be revealed before a different approach can be taken. It took time for Lluvi to recognize this one and many others. Had she paid more attention to Darryl and communicated her needs prior to this, there's a greater possibility that this uproar would not have happened.

The value Darryl places on sleep is higher than Lluvi's. His level of appreciation for it superseded her understanding. Darryl had not been able to get a full night's sleep since he was 15 years old. Once he and his sisters and niece were removed from his parents' home a new level of alertness immediately developed.

His head was now on a swivel while being in the temporary group home with his 8 year old sister (his 17 year old sister and her 14 month old daughter were separated and taken to a different group home). When Darryl now rests his eyes he is looking forward to as much sleep as he can and treasures it more than Lluvi can understand.

Although cautious not to wake Darryl up, she didn't realize the severity this would cause. Waking up to his arm bending the wrong way caused Darryl to ignite in self defense and protection mode. Knowing it was his wife and not an intruder it was his words and not his hands that went up swinging to protect himself. Things subsided as Darryl and Lluvi continued to try to love each other the best they could and as much as the other would allow the love.

10/11/06 10:38am

I wake up to the presence of a cold bed
I reach for him to cuddle and rest my head
I am pushed away, rejected and sat aside
I pretend things are fine, but really I run and hide
I worry on the future that lies ahead
I want to be set free and just rest my head

Life continued with brutal injuries to both Darryl and Lluvi as they both attempted to preserve themselves from each other's harmful attacks. They continued going to church in hopes something would change, but although they were being fed God's word from the pastor on the pulpit, they were on their own at home to face each other's vicious insults.

One Sunday morning, Darryl and Lluvi's pastor,

Jerry Dirmann, was announcing a 4 week intense discipleship program their church, The Rock, was offering. Darryl began to consider taking this course. His heart was stirring.

"This is exactly what I need to get closer to God; to hear His voice clearer," he thought. He felt lost in his marriage. He could see Lluvi leaving him if things didn't change. She brought up divorce often. Divorce was on the horizon for Lluvi and he didn't want to lose her again. He just didn't know what changes were ever going to be good enough for her. He felt like he could never be who she wanted him to be. He just didn't see himself as enough for her.

They had drifted and gone off course so quickly and they needed to find their sense of direction again. Hopeful that this program could be what they needed, he bravely approached Lluvi after service. With some effort, he convinced Lluvi to take it with him.

Reluctantly, she agreed to give this 4 week journey a try. Living with Darryl, she learned how to sniff out manipulation, but she couldn't figure Darryl out at the moment. Was he sincere in his desire to grow closer in his walk with God or was it all a ploy so she could back off and no longer interrogate him through his lies? She was exhausted from always having to be alert to his deceptions. Weariness was weighing heavy on her heart and mind.

Darryl had started his career in sales at 16. Lluvi grew to understand his sales tactics. From the vocabulary he would use to the pauses he would have to buy himself time to think through his next steps; she knew them. He practiced on her plenty. She was in tune to his profession and recognized his methods. She did not want to be sold. She was tired of Darryl trying to sell her a lie. She just wanted authenticity from him. She just wanted him to be real and not glamorize himself with false advertisement. She was tired of being deceived.

She was not at her best during her run-down moments with him. When she lacked energy, this ogre-like monster would emerge from her very soul. She hated herself in that form. She hated Darryl for pushing her to that edge. She hated everything.

Hate was a new friend who found a home in her dark cold mansion that protected her against Darryl. Hate would somehow ease the pain she felt right before sadness would morph into anger. Neither of those emotions were present at that moment though. Confusion was staring her in the face at that moment.

Confusion was always there when there was a whirlwind of emotions cycloning themselves around her. But today, confusion was there alone. Alone with her. Confusion was face to face with her; questioning reality with her. Whether this was a manipulation tactic or not, she was hopeful that she would draw closer to God. She was determined to focus on God through these next four weeks.

On May 20, 2007, Lluvi nervously entered the room where the church's discipleship course would take place. Darryl seemed calm and collected to her. He always had that appearance around people though; as if nothing ever bothered him. It was at times annoying to her. Today was no exception.

During the class's orientation, Lluvi's reluctancy changed from hesitant to "oh bleep what did I sign up for!" Yes, there's a "bleep" in this PG-rated version. Lluvi was in shock at hearing of all the restrictions those 4 weeks would hold.

For 4 weeks, Lluvi would have to limit her media time. Two hours of tv, movies, internet, etc per week! "What is that all about?!" She wondered. This by far was the weirdest thing one would sign up for. Lluvi looked at Darryl. He read her shocked face, but quickly dismissed it.

Darryl's foster dad, Gary, had spoken highly about this program and encouraged them to take it. Darryl was willing to sacrifice his media intake if it meant fixing his marriage. Lluvi's 23 year old mind could not imagine this being their fix-all; if anything, without her pacifier of a TV and computer this had the potential to separate them even further.

She sat quietly listening to both her thoughts and the voice in front of the room going over the class. At the sound of the rules to the program, she sensed control peaking out in alertness ready to pounce at any given opportunity. She did not want to give power to someone else and yet there she sat quietly determined to submit. She desperately wanted her marriage to work and if Darryl was willing to walk this out, then she would follow suit. They were both unprepared for what would transpire from this program.

Chapter 11

OPERATION SOLID LIVES

The Operation Solid Lives (OSL) program was more than what both Darryl and Lluvi expected it to be. Reading the Bible and journaling daily, listening to multiple messages per week while taking notes, attending mid-week and Sunday service, again, while taking notes, serving in a weekly ministry, along with all the restrictions was intense. And yet through the process, Lluvi learned it was doable.

Lluvi didn't realize just how much time she had until she eliminated all the excess media and entertainment time. During the final week prior to graduating the course, she began to recognize the shift that had taken place in her heart. She didn't feel bound to media like she had at the start of class. This new found realization that life not only exists without this, but can flourish by cutting out media held freedom that was once unrecognizable nor unattainable.

Both Darryl and Lluvi could now recognize and pinpoint things that were unnecessary to have in life. Was watching TV evil? No. But it was a distraction that withheld them from drawing closer to one another. It prevented them from addressing things head on and enabled them to continue to sweep things under the rug. They couldn't be fully present toward each other if they were constantly seeking to be entertained. It was an avoidance behavior, they didn't even know existed within them.

The last class was set up as a potluck feast to celebrate the students in their journey. Students were made known that there was time set apart for students to share their testimonies. Lluvi knew exactly what she wanted to share, if she could build confidence to take the mic. The past four weeks had wrecked her in the most beautiful way. She didn't know it was possible to experience being wrecked in a positive way. Up until that point she saw it as destructive process. Although this messy and crumbling process is exactly what took place, it did not feel dreadful as Lluvi's world came to an end.

"The world and everything in it that I knew to be and brought life to me, is now exposed as a lie," Lluvi reflected. "This class revealed the truth about what fulfillment of life looks like." Both Darryl and Lluvi understood that they were always striving and attempting to make their relationship work. It was focused on each other instead of what it means to be intertwined with God as their covenant mark on their arms displayed.

Life during this class was no longer focused on how to fix their marriage. It was no longer focused on Darryl and Lluvi, but instead life. Life for Darryl and God and life for Lluvi and God. The unity that began to form within their marriage those past four weeks was the byproduct of abiding in and connecting with God individually. It was no longer about Darryl and Lluvi and yet, by releasing that focus, God was able to unite Darryl and Lluvi at a new level. Interestingly, by releasing what they thought they were to focus on allowed their hearts to tenderize toward the Lord and they found themselves closer to one another.

At the end of the course, they were presented with the opportunity to continue and take the second course. There were a total of six courses in this program. The first course was four weeks, but the rest were each six weeks long. Confident in the potential this next class held, enthusiastically they signed up.

One of the requirements within the courses was to serve in a ministry. Darryl saw leaders playing basketball with kids while checking in their son for Kids Church. He suggested to Lluvi that they serve in that age group. Lluvi was hoping to be around kids that didn't really talk or ask questions about the Bible. Although she feared moments would arise, she unenthusiastically signed up with her husband.

They began serving the 4th through 6th graders of their church. Darryl found himself in his element; having fun. It was as if he was one of the kids himself. Lluvi found herself many times stretched out of her comfort zone.

Being in ministry forced them to work together at a new level. As friction between them continued to disintegrate, it became enjoyable for both to work alongside each other. They began to understand one another more and more by each passing week.

Over time, they were leading the service with a team that consisted of more teenagers than adults to love these 4th-6th graders. They spent their time planning meetings, events, services, and growing closer to God. As they continued to draw closer to God, they were drawing closer to each other.

Life was not perfect and disagreements still took place, but extending grace and mercy toward each other grew to new heights. They began to understand how to best partner with one another. They began to pick up on each other's shortcomings and strengthen those areas of weakness instead of picking them apart and devaluing one another. They were becoming each other's number one fan.

Darryl was becoming more and more familiar with Lluvi's behavior when her stress level would begin to rise. Before, he would avoid her and do his best to let her be and ignore her. This time around, with a more tender heart, he offered his help and possibly at times solutions, if Lluvi was open to them.

Lluvi was becoming more aware of Darryl's needs. His need to have fun had been overlooked as Lluvi had originally thought it as unimportant. Although Lluvi is more serious than Darryl, she needed to join him in the fun and silliness life had to offer. He enjoyed her that way. They began new fun ways of connecting.

Every now and again, either one would say a sentence and then another that rhymed with the last word of the first sentence. If Lluvi started it, then Darryl would chime in and throw in a sentence to rhyme to Lluvi's sentence while keeping the theme of the conversation. Their days were more interesting that way. It brought laughter and a new level of closeness through witty rhyming sentences. Laughter is the new found remedy they needed while still going through the realities to the challenges their marriage continued to face.

Throughout the next few years and multiple classes taken through this six level discipleship program, brought Lluvi to many moments of pondering. Lluvi sat staring at her Bible perplexed one day. She realized that although she had given Jesus permission to be the Lord over her life the day she accepted Him as Lord and Savior, at times she behaved as if that were not true.

Although Lluvi loved connecting with God and talking to Him throughout her day, she realized that through timed prayer and her ignorance she was being shortchanged. "This new structured way to pray is hard," she voiced her dissatisfaction to God. "I just want to talk to You," she continued. "Am I really not using my prayer time effectively, Daddy?" she questioned. In her fear of disappointing God and her pastors, she continued abiding with the class requirements.

Through her timed prayer, Lluvi became more and more aware that she was walking through the motions to say she did it, but she was feeling more and more distant from God. If she stopped, "would it limit my spiritual growth?" she questioned herself. Twenty-five minutes seemed like an hour when Lluvi did not know what to talk about. Prior to OSL classes, she enjoyed her time talking to God, but now realized that a more structured prayer time discombobulated her. She was unsure of how to behave. She discerned that this part was similar to how people feel when learning their manners.

As babies and toddlers, we communicate our needs and wants for our parents to provide. As we get older, we begin to learn the mannerism we need to include in our requests and conversations with our parents. In confusion, Lluvi was trying to understand if she was now leaving her Christian baby/toddler stage and developing into the next level of her Christian walk. It felt uncomfortable and foreign to pray the way she was being taught. Still, she loved God and was willing to embrace learning the mannerism she needed to express love to her Abba

Father.

Sadness was leading her to a new place of loneliness. She was discovering that she could no longer approach God like a baby does. Babies cry to communicate to their parents their needs; be it hunger or discomfort, etc. They only have one form of communicating needs. Instead, she sensed she was expanding her vocabulary and learning to ask politely to be fed or needing comfort. Fear of making mistakes or doing things wrong hung in the back of her mind. She didn't want to disappoint God as He taught her these new ways of living as His follower.

In all her confusion, she continued to love God and continue this program. Not only did Lluvi's new prayer experiences challenge her, she was now also able to recognize just how poisonous doubt can be in her prayers to God. Doubt has the power to ruin a well articulated prayer.

Doubt is the key ingredient to an unsuccessful prayer. Doubt is the difference between a wish and prayer. This frightened Lluvi. "What if I doubt?!" she feared silently. "Life is hard, God. I'm afraid I won't always have the faith for things when it gets hard. I know hard, Daddy. I know life is not easy. We're living with my parents because things are hard." she cried out.

"I want to believe for my promise land and a home we can call our own, but what if I doubt? Oh Daddy!" she wailed. In fear that her prayers would go unanswered, she worried and allowed these thoughts to consume her.

"A faith-filled sentence is the power behind the activation of the prayer" the teachings continued week after week. Lluvi began to understand the many forms of prayer a little more clearly. Similar to a lightbulb and a switch to turn it on, the power comes from the electricity that drives the light bulb to turn on. A prayer is the lightbulb, she is the switch, but her faith is the electrical current that activates her prayers to see results.

Without this electrical current, the light bulb does not function properly. "Without faith my prayers are not activated?" she chewed on this teaching. A new revelation hit her! "I do have faith! I believe You, God! I believe in Your power because of who You are!" Lluvi exclaimed in a new found peace. Worry was fleeing as peace filled her heart and mind.

"Prayer is a conversation with God," was being confirmed through her classes. "That's right! That's what I've been doing this whole time," Lluvi argued silently. "Prayer is a lifetime behavior for a believer. Ephesian 6:18 says Christians are to be praying always in the Spirit. Always praying means always in communication with God.

1 Thessalonians 5:17 tells believers to pray without ceasing. Those words were resonating in Lluvi's heart as she gained more and more understanding. As she listened to the prayer teachings, she concluded that prayer is to spirituality as love is to marriage. "Prayer is what increases and

deepens my relationship with God," she rested assured.

Through the classes, Darryl and Lluvi were being taught that prayer can be much more than they had thought it was. At first setting her timer and attempting to just sit and talk to God for the allotted time was scary. She would run out of things to talk about and found herself praying for things to fill the time. The thought of having filler prayers disgusted her. She didn't want her talks with God to consist of time fillers. She began to mourn her once love filled prayers to God throughout her days.

One teaching set her free from her once time filling prayers. Lluvi found hope as she learned that prayer includes "praise, worship, thanksgiving, consecration (not my will but His will), praise of petitions (requests), supplication (humbly and earnestly), and repentance, listening to God's voice" (Dirmann, 2009). She now understood that she could sing to God or read the Bible and fill in her name and make His word personalized for her life. She was gaining new levels of understanding to the once dreadful requirement to fill.

When her pastors began to dissect each type of prayer, excitement filled her heart in knowing she could use all these different types of prayers in her daily class requirements. Understanding that praise prayers give God glory brought an interesting feeling of freedom. She wasn't feeling the restrictions any longer.

Psalm 150 tells Christians to: "Let all things praise the Lord. Praise the Lord! Praise God in His sanctuary; praise Him in His mighty firmament! Praise Him for His mighty acts; praise Him according to His excellent greatness! Praise Him with the sound of the trumpet; praise Him with the lute and harp!" Praise can be done through song and sounds of instruments. "What!? I don't even have to speak?" knowing this blew Lluvi's mind. Lluvi doesn't know how to play an instrument, but somehow she started to understand that she is that instrument. Just like King David, she can dance in rejoicing God's goodness and that's considered a form of praise.

What used to confuse Lluvi, was becoming more clear. Praise and worship differ, but she had not understood how they differed up until these courses. "Praise is about God, worship is to God. Praise is opening up, worship is entering in. Praise is boldly declaring, worship is humbly bowing in the presence of a Holy God. Praise applauds what God has done, worship is honoring God for who He is" (Winkler, 2017). Brooke Ligertwood says it this way, "Praise has a sound, but worship has an aroma" (Ligertwood, 2023).

More and more, both Darryl and Lluvi continued to grow in their understanding of prayer and the vast parts that it could entail. They learned that listening to God is part of prayer, as it is in any conversation. "One-way conversations are not fitting for her marriage, so likewise, neither are one-way conversations fitting for the development and growth in my relationship with God," Lluvi grasped.

She didn't feel like she was discounting the importance of listening, but it was clear that through her belief that her 20 minute prayer time she perceived it was all her doing the talking. She was taking it all in in hopes to be a better Christian; one that God was pleased with. "It is crucial I deepen my relationship with You, God," she whispered in desperation.

The heavy weight of finding things to talk about was a thing of the past and no longer part of her future. Lluvi now felt the encouragement to be still, sit and allow God to respond. It is the key to heeding His direction. Afterall, how can she walk out the direction He's leading if she can't hear Him.

"Without this ability to be still and hear God's responses, following His leading will continue to feel blurry and questionable," Lluvi was beginning to understand. "It is like trying to tune a radio station that keeps coming in with static," she heard her pastor say. "I might be able to make out what is being spoken, but I will still need to fill in a lot of the blanks," Lluvi concluded. Filling in the blanks has the potential to misunderstand God's precise leading and within the incorrect timing," Lluvi now understood. "Taking the time to speak to God and listen to Him is needed in order to walk out a fulfilling life," she concluded.

After learning of the different forms of prayer,

Lluvi's prayer life was not only pleasant, but fulfilling. It was more exciting and joyful. A new sense of delight wrapped around her heart. Her connection with God grew in a way that at times she felt umbilical corded to Him. (Umbilical corded is not a term, until we make it. Let's make it one). Lluvi could feel herself being nourished and nurtured in such a precise and direct way. Through daily prayer it felt like there was no separation between God and Lluvi. Nothing could separate them from each other.

Lluvi took what she learned from the prayer teachings and was now applying the additional methods in her precious prayer time. Lluvi used God's Word to pray over her marriage and the people she loved. She read God's word and declared them in faith.

The faith-filled prayers held such power that she began to meditate on specific scriptures and see God's word as more powerful than her circumstances. Writing in her journal allowed her thoughts and fears to be overpowered by God's word. It was as if writing out the circumstance while adding the scripture, she felt led to write, would somehow trump her situation.

Some results were not always visible to neither Darryl nor Lluvi, and yet they continued this path of pursuing God more and more eagerly. "Why is this marriage so difficult?" they would at times both think. "Why couldn't they just love each other and live happily ever after?" was the question bellowing in Lluvi's mind.

In the midst of Lluvi's hidden pain, she continued applying what OSL had taught her. There were times Lluvi was full of sorrow and distraught. Her prayer journal was the tool that allowed her to regain her strength. She would pull out her prayer journal countless times and read her written prayers to proclaim God's truths over her family and marriage.

She added to the prayer journal other personalized scripture prayers over other situations as well. In her Bible readings she found a scripture that popped out of the page. "God restores the years the locust have eaten" (Joel 2:25). Hope filled every part of her being as she reread that phrase over and over. This became her marriage scripture that brought a new level of faith.

"God is a God of restoration!" she proclaimed. This new found promise was quoted over and over from her lips. It began to dissolve and embed in every fiber of her heart and become one within her. She believed God to restore the years the locust had eaten within her relationship with Darryl. "Every single locust-destroyed moment was going to be restored!" She sang forth proclaiming this new found truth for her life. Then all of a sudden memories flooded her brain.

She resisted entertaining them for fear she would fall into the traps of jealousy once again. "Darryl is not that person" she argued within herself. "Darryl hasn't been that person," she continued. "Maybe, but that doesn't mean he isn't capable of falling," she heard that familiar voice. She knew this voice all too well. Behind this voice was one who came only to kill, steal, and destroy her life. She needed to combat him, but was falling weak at the ringing of his words. She feared Darryl would fall into temptation. She feared she still wasn't enough for him. She feared her abrupt moments of control, anger and jealousy would question Darryl's ability to tough this out.

She spoke with the depth of her core, "NO! Darryl is a new creation, old things have passed away, behold all things have become new!" sounded the words from her lips. "I know how to make him stumble; I know his weaknesses," she heard the eerie voice again. "God's greater than his weaknesses," she boldly proclaimed. "He who is in Darryl is greater than he who is in the world," rang through her home.

Faith was springing forth in the midst of these daggers attacking her thoughts. She knew how big her God is, she knew His love for her. She knew Him. Not just about Him; Lluvi knew God and His character. She nestled safe in God's peace after winning that battle knowing in the back of her mind that she would need to continue her training to win the future battles.

Mark 4:15 shot up in her mind. Her pastor had been teaching on this all throughout his Sunday services. "And these are the ones by the wayside where the word is sown. When they hear, Satan comes immediately and takes away the word that was sown in their hearts." "Ohhh! The devil is scared," she thought. "Immediately he came Daddy," she said as she connected with God about that moment. "He's sneaky, isn't he?" she continued. She could almost feel God's embrace. Without any more words being said, she felt His tender love.

In the intense moments and the good moments, Lluvi would use the journal daily to proclaim God's word and truth. This allowed her to hold fast to God's truth over what she saw, heard, thought or felt. This prayer journal positioned her to stand in faith for what God had promised. It helped her to magnify God instead of magnifying her situations.

This prayer journal empowered Lluvi to walk by faith and not by sight. In some of her darkest moments where fear tried to cripple her and silence her, she applied what she had learned and used her prayer tools to gain her confidence and strength. One prayer journal became two, then three, then four, and so on. These journals continued to get filled with her writings. These prayer journals became the tool she needed to believe God for the impossible. It is as if it reignited a fire in her soul to push through her fear and doubt-filled thoughts. It lifted her up to believe God over what she saw in the natural.

The days continued. And walking out what she learned from OSL became more and more applicable. Protecting her heart was also taught within the OSL program. At first Lluvi didn't quite understand this concept. She had heard her whole life to follow her heart and now she was hearing that it is not biblical.

Jeremiah 17:9 says, "The heart is deceitful above all things, and desperately wicked: who can know it?" Even though the heart is deceitful we must protect our hearts from the power to deceive us.

Throughout the OSL classes Darryl and Lluvi had certain intangible requirements on their checklist. They are as follows:

☑ "I have intentionally been loving and encouraging to those around me."
☑ "I have been an example of what a disciple should be."
☑ "I have spent adequate quality time with my family this week."
☑ "I have been a servant to my leaders."
☑ "I have kept myself from distractions and have abstained from more than one hour of secular media."

There were times that Lluvi checked the boxes in front of these statements and there were times that she did not. Protecting her heart is based on limiting the amount of "junk" intake.

Having only one hour of media such as television, internet, books, newspapers, video games, etc. was not an easy task for her through those early moments of disciplining herself in this area. In the beginning, Lluvi found this to be extremely difficult. She was used to all those things filling up her day. By removing these distractions she was able to focus on the other aspects the classes directed.

Throughout those classes, Lluvi had one hour per week for levels 2-6 to check her social media accounts, listen to secular music, read up on current events etc. Sixty minutes didn't seem very long for this, but towards the middle of the program, she found herself not using the hour she did have. No longer was she watching the many episodes of her favorite television shows.

In between courses with the requirements lifted, she attempted to return to her old lifestyle, but only to find that she could not sit through the shows she once enjoyed. They were full of inappropriate scenes she had not noticed before. The language used was foul with many innuendos. These entertaining episodes and movies were forming her mindsets in particular topics.

"It has the ability to shape my thinking." she excitedly understood. Prior to taking OSL, she had not noticed all the "junk" she was taking in. In listening to these teachings, it was as if scales were falling from Lluvi's eyes. Excited that now she had the ability to see more clearly, she accepted this new lighter way to walk with God.

Darryl and Lluvi began to refrain from what they used to watch on the screens and what they used to listen to on the radio. In the OSL classes, they were taught that they feed their hearts daily through what they see and hear. "Wow! All these years, what have I been feeding myself?" Lluvi wondered while taking notes in her class.

The music on the radio although they have great rhythms and beats have words that dishonor God.

"I've been dishonoring You, Daddy?" with sorrow in her heart, Lluvi began to understand. "Singing along to these songs has caused me to regurgitate what I have been listening to and has been filling my heart with it," wowed Lluvi in awe of this new profound insight.

Darryl and Lluvi were taught through these classes that out of the abundance of their hearts, their mouths speak (Matthew 12:34). They were also taught that the more they fed themselves such junk, the more they were going to pour out this same junk throughout their days. A lightbulb stood above Darryl and Lluvi through this new realization. "Had this been a culprit in their marriage?" They pondered.

Afterall, they had been spewing out and dumping junk on one another through their words. Lluvi pictured it to be similar to food fights leaving one another all slimed up and filthy with a limited ability to walk away clean. They had been doing to one another–but worse!; She now knew there had been toxins in their ammo that seeped into the core of each other's being.

Over the years of being at their church, both Darryl and Lluvi recognized their behavior shifted. They realized that the more and more that they disciplined themselves to refrain from going over their one hour of media each week, the more and more their desire for such media decreased. They realized the difference of what they used to value versus what they were beginning to value. They recognized their newfound love and hunger for God's Word. While reading His Word they grasped that it was not only His Word they appreciated, but that a desire for His presence was rapidly increasing.

Since separating themselves from the filth the certain entertainment brought forth, they recognized the behavioral differences of one another. Through those scales that were falling from their eyes, they could recognize that God's Word was cleansing them. This cleansing was the help they both needed. It felt almost like a literal shower that cleansed and refreshed them. Subsequently, they no longer held this desire to go back in the mud. They now were enjoying the feeling of being clean over the feeling of being muddied up. This profound recognition brought forth new freedoms from this abounding truth.

During those classes, Darryl and Lluvi also realized that what they fed themselves determined the direction of life. A new level of understanding was shedding light to areas they had not thought of prior to the classes. They now understood that their behavior has a deep correlation to what they "feed" themselves. As they detached from certain movies, Lluvi recognized that romantic comedies affected her marriage. She realized that she would compare her precious husband to the main character and hope and wish for him to treat her like the lovers would in those movies. The more they fed themselves wholesome nourishing media, the more they realized the effect the "junk" media had on their lives and view on marriage in general.

Darryl and Lluvi were now obtaining the ability to see and differentiate the difference between junk intake and nourishment from God's truth. As discernment continued to increase the dangers of living in a box and removing themselves from society alerted them to the dangers of being legalistic. "Protecting our heart does not mean to bubble wrapping ourselves from the filth of the world," they discussed together. "It means to cleanse ourselves with God's Word daily so that the junk does not latch on to us," they concluded. The tool their marriage needed was now at their fingertips. Learning to use this tool would take practice, but they were determined to walk this out together.

The New Living Translation says "Guard your heart above all else, for it determines the course of your life (Proverbs 4:23). The New King James Version states it this way: "Keep your heart with all diligence, for out of it spring the issues of life" (Proverbs 4:23). To guard, protect and keep their hearts required a deeper understanding of why they must do so. The "why" drives a person's what.

Proverbs 23:7 says, "For as he thinks in his heart, so is he." This means that their non-physical hearts are the emotions wrapped up in their thinking. Darryl & Lluvi's thinking is the steering wheel to their lives. Their thoughts whether positive, negative, good, or bad have a way of controlling their attitude.

"Your attitudes are the sum total of your thoughts. Your attitudes lead to your actions" (Rogers, 2019). Darryl and Lluvi's thoughts inevitably lead their behavior. They cannot just by pure desire stop thinking a certain way. Mindsets have been formed and developed over time. They each had years of learning how to think. Changing their mindsets requires a new set of patterns and habits.

The Operation Solid Lives's program was set up to help Darryl and Lluvi redirect thoughts. It is set up to activate Romans 12:2 in their lives. Romans 12:2 says, "Do not be conformed to this world, but be transformed by the renewing of your mind, that you may prove what is that good and acceptable and perfect will of God." A transformation takes place when they allow the infiltration of the Word of God to shape their thoughts.

The Word of God is powerful. It is not mere letters turned into words in a language that they were reading, but instead it was penetrating their soul and spirit as they continued to hear the spoken Word of God. Hebrews 4:12 says, "For the word of God is alive and active. Sharper than any double-edged sword, it penetrates even to divide soul and spirit, joints and marrow; it judges the thoughts and attitudes of the heart."

"The Word of God has the power to transform our lives," Lluvi sat in awe of God's beautiful love to not leave them the way they were. "God is willing to walk with us through this process so patiently," she continued. "Transformation should not be mistaken with change," rang in her ears. Darryl and Lluvi had gathered a new level of understanding that set up the trajectory for their lives.

Change modifies behavior. Transformation modifies belief systems and values. Change happens in a more external fashion. Transformation is internal resulting with external and visible byproducts. Both Darryl and Lluvi were willing to go through the transformation process. They were tired of behavioral modification that did not seem to stand against misunderstandings and disagreements.

Chapter 12

A LURED HEART

On a daily basis, Darryl and Lluvi continued to practice what they had learned through the teachings from their church. Life was taking on a new form for them both individually and collectively.

Lluvi's past desire to *never* be pregnant again faded. The aversion of experiencing another pregnancy was now transposed to a new desire to be pregnant. This new desire was new to both Darryl and Lluvi and yet they both knew that God was going to restore this experience for them both. They felt as if they were getting a second chance to love one another through this beautiful experience of bringing forth a baby in this world.

Month after month and year after year came negative pregnancy tests. Surely, Lluvi was fertile. Zaqry was proof of that. And yet, disappointment each month began to sneak in to question God's goodness. They committed to remain steadfast and pray for their redemptive pregnancy.

They did not lose heart and continued to believe God to restore the years the locust had eaten. In the waiting, they continued to serve in kids church and summer camps. In their leadership roles, meeting many wonderful people at church came naturally. In all the beauty that was springing forth from their marriage, Lluvi found herself in a predicament she never expected to face.

Their little family of 3 became friends with many different families from the church. On one of their visits to a certain family's home. Lluvi found herself drawn to this young man. They shared a birthday together which sparked conversation. Thinking nothing of it, they continued to visit that family who had that friend over when they would visit. They spent significant time with this family and their friend. They enjoyed their company and went on different family outings. This built many memories together from many dinners together to a full day at Disneyland. The more time they spent, the more their friendships with this family blossomed.

One evening while at their friends' home, Lluvi sat comfortably on their couch with their friends' daughters and their family friend. Darryl and their friends were in the kitchen cooking and conversing. Fear stabbed Lluvi that evening. She was struck with the oddest feelings.

This young man who sat next to her was asking her all the right questions. Whether he realized it or not, he was luring her heart. Up until that point, she had not found this young man attractive. "What was going on!?" she wondered. "Darryl and I have a good marriage!" she argued internally. "Why is this guy now intriguing her?" she wondered. She awkwardly and generously answered his questions about herself.

"Why did I feel cared for with this guy?" she asked herself. "I love Darryl," she reminded herself. "So why did it feel so good to have this guy want to get to know me," she was baffled and scared. "Could it be that Darryl doesn't pursue you any longer?" came that familiar voice. With a sad sigh, she took the bait, "yeah," she answered.

"Darryl doesn't want to get to know me anymore," she sorrowfully realized. She began seeing this young man's face in admiration. Her mind was trailing a new path for her thoughts to lead her. She was anticipating for the next time they would talk. This young man was warm and caring with a heart to get to know her. The *her* that doesn't seem to interest Darryl any longer. As easy as that, she was lured into emotional infidelity.

Battling her new found desire to be pursued, she raged against herself. Hatred for her foolishness would take a hold of her as if to choke her. She combatted her desires by reminding herself of her love for Darryl. When Darryl and Lluvi argued (because there are always disagreements between a husband and wife), she reverted back into this weird fantasy that she had the potential to be pursued.

Oh how she wished Darryl would be the pursuer. Instead, Darryl seemed so satisfied with the state of their marriage. He didn't seem fazed by the lack of romance. While she now craved for more, his contentment caused her emotions to be drawn toward this other young man. In fear of what this would lead to she did one of the bravest things to do in that time.

Lluvi called her friend, Rachel, whom she met during their OSL classes. They scheduled a time to meet up. As they walked her friend's neighborhood, she confessed her unfathomable secret. This friend was no ordinary friend. This friend made a vow to be her covenant friend. Meaning, Rachel committed to asking Lluvi the difficult questions that not everyone gets the privilege to know. Lluvi shared the details of how this came about and how it had been eating at her for the past couple of weeks.

Rachel, being the covenant friend that she was, encouraged her to tell her husband. Freaking out, Lluvi looked through her files of thoughts for another possible solution only to find none that would bring the freedom she needed–the freedom her marriage needed. The freedom only found through transparency was in its infancy stages of forming and developing within Darryl and Lluvi's marriage. It was not fully cured nor ready for the weight of life's marital challenges to set foot on.

"Could this destroy our marriage," Lluvi wondered in fear. Rachel reassured her that it would not be easy, but it would bring them the breakthrough they needed. Lluvi could not comprehend this exhaustive concept.

"How could revealing this possibly bring them a breakthrough?" she questioned within herself. Rachel is 10 years her senior with beautiful maturity in this area. She held great wisdom that day. Yet, little did Rachel know how her words would impact Darryl and Lluvi's future.

Later that week Lluvi found the courage and right timing to break the news of this emotional betrayal she committed. It was no easy task to determine the best timing and yet, she knew she couldn't wait any longer; plus Rachel was continuously following up to ensure Lluvi was held accountable.

This news did not reach Darryl's ears with the same peace Lluvi felt in exposing her secret. He looked at her intently. Once the shock wore off, he was just as confused as to how she could have experienced this. Anger against this young man was met with Lluvi's words of tranquility. "He doesn't know he's caused this in my heart, babe. I don't think he had bad intentions. I think he was just being nice. He didn't know his friendliness would have this effect on me. Remember, he's waiting for his girlfriend to return from her internship next year," she assured Darryl. Evenstill, Darryl felt like a cannonball shot him in the stomach.

Darryl now had a close eye on Lluvi. Lluvi now made it a point to side-hug those of the opposite gender. They were both determined to keep Lluvi out of the possibility of this recurring with anyone else. They began to distance themselves from their friends if they knew of the young man's participation.

As Lluvi felt gawked at by Darryl, it began to increase a new level of uncertainty and her confidence dwindled. She was now cautious of her every move around the opposite sex. She now lived in a place of exhaustion from being on high alert. Even if she knew nothing would ever happen with whatever man was in front of her, she remained cautious which awkwardly communicated that she might be covering up feelings for them. It brought more awkwardness and confusion to everyone involved.

It was not all bad, though. This positioned Darryl to also confide in his covenant friend, Jesse, Rachel's husband. Darryl felt reassured of the safety to expose his deep, dark secrets. Realizing how free he was feeling, he allowed his covenant friend to ask the difficult questions. The ones that check his heart and its intentions.

Vulnerability had never been part of neither Darryl nor Lluvi's vocabulary. They had been professional deceivers only looking to protect themselve. Now, through Lluvi's exposed blindspot, they were entering a new level in their marriage. They were allowing vulnerability to have its way in their lives and marriage. Vulnerability exposes deception. Freedom was on the horizon for both Darryl and Lluvi. Both separately and collectively as husband and wife.

As time progressed and Lluvi continued her new life pattern of alertness and guarded ways, she began to see an increase of her desire to be pregnant. In desperation, she went to a healing service her church was having. She had never witnessed people falling on the floor before. It looked a bit scary and not approachable. Darryl led her down the aisle so she could walk by the man from India who came to preach, teach and heal those that night. She heard him praying and he touched her forehead. She felt no different and was thankful she didn't fall to the ground wailing as she walked by those doing so. She didn't feel any different. She didn't sense a change. She wasn't sure what to make of this, but continued her days with God and her family.

One day, later that summer Lluvi felt prompted to take a pregnancy test. The air was warm with a slight breeze as she entered her friend's house ready to pee on that stick. This time seeing a positive pregnancy test came with such joy and no sorrow in sight. "We are finally going to walk out restoration in this area that once held deep wounds," she excitedly thought.

The pregnancy was different than they had both expected. Her previous years fighting bulimia could not have prepared her for this. Lluvi had never wished so desperately that she could just vomit.

Unfortunately, she couldn't. Her stomach always seemed empty and everything disgusted her. Darryl's now sweet tender love protruded from his being to ensure his wife felt cared for through this process of having his baby. He went to get her specific foods in hopes she'd eat. He finished her food when she couldn't. He rubbed her feet when they were swollen and positioned himself to support her back throughout the long nights of discomfort for Lluvi.

Although the pregnancy held many physical and emotional difficulties, Lluvi was met with the power of love and support. Lluvi found comfort in her friends who too were on this pregnancy journey. Jessica made Lluvi a pregnancy calendar of beautiful encouragements throughout every page. Yecenia offered her support to help Lluvi find an OBGYN that didn't push for another C-section like her existing doctor. Teena walked alongside helping Lluvi find her taste buds again and opening up her world to Vietnamese food. Lluvi felt love from all her friends who expressed their joy for the prayer come true.

Darryl Lluvi's redemption baby was on its way! Again, it was not an easy pregnancy in the physical form, but that was overlooked by the power of love and the wealth of emotional support Lluvi felt from Darryl. It was physically exhausting for both, but emotionally rewarding for each of them.

On February of 2011, Zhandyn was born to non-teenage parents who love and care for one another deeper than they had before. Having their little family of four in that hospital room brought such peace & tranquility in their hearts. Zaqry was shy of 10 years old. And baby duties had been far behind them but they embraced the sleepless nights with joy at the unity they held through the restoration and healing God was bringing forth.

As life continued and their boys continued to grow and mature, Darryl and Lluvi taught their boys the important aspects they had learned through their time at The Rock. Since their boys were little, guarding and protecting their hearts was as natural as keeping their physical bodies clean and maintaining proper hygiene. There have been many instances at the stores where they are walking from one department to another and their sons bounced their eyes after being met with posters of half-naked women in the undergarments department.

They had instilled in them to protect their hearts from the perversity the world had created. They themselves can now recognize the "junk" that infiltrates the world. Darryl and Lluvi continued to have conversations about the sacredness of marriage. As they matured more and more each day, their boys began to have a better understanding of the "why" behind protecting their hearts.

"It is not only for their sake, but for their future wife and family," they'd hear their parents often say. For Darryl and Lluvi to see their boys bounce their eyes on their own was bringing reassurance that they were understanding the "why." This means that it is not just an external behavior, but an internal transformation is taking place.

Each day Darryl and Lluvi were faced with protecting their hearts. Not only from explicit billboards, but from anything that tried to distract them from walking worthy of their calling, which is to love God and people–they were each other's people. They learned that things can be permissible, but not all things are profitable.

During their time in youth ministry they created an object lesson using a balloon and shaving cream. Darryl filled the balloon up with shaving cream, tied it and asked their youth what would come out if he popped the balloon. They all told him that shaving cream would come out. He demonstrated this very example and popped the balloon forcing shaving cream to explode from the balloon. He then relayed the message about the importance of guarding our hearts from being filled with junk. Darryl concluded the object lesson with the scripture, Matthew 12:34, "For out of the abundance of the heart the mouth speaks." Darryl and Lluvi reminded them that our words lead to actions; our action leads to patterns and habits; and our habits direct our lives. The issues of life reflect what we are filling our hearts with.

Lluvi continued to battle against jealousy. She was determined to win. Jealousy was very persistent to berate Lluvi's mind. She knew that once she entertained these thoughts and allowed them to stay, they would take over. Darryl traveled for work and was around many attractive women. Lluvi would put on 10 pounds a year as her winter coat. She feared Darryl would one day find her to have been "false advertisement" from what her younger 16 year old body was like.

The importance of her physical appearance would swing like a pendulum. When her heart safely trusted Darryl, she would eat whatever and be at peace with what she looked like. When she found Darryl distant and disengaged in their marriage, she feared her body size was the determining factor to his disconnectedness. As silly as it might sound, those were the lies she believed. And again at war with lies she vulnerably positioned herself for attacks and future defeats.

One rainy morning she drove and parked outside a familiar building. The rain had now stopped. As she sat waiting in her car while Zaqry, who now went by Zaq, took high school enrichment class through their local homeschool co-op, she drifted off into thought. She felt God gently speak as she silently looked at the trees in front of her. Although the clouds covered the sun that brisk autumn day, it did not feel like a gloomy morning. As she looked at the almost bare trees, she saw leaves dancing around going from her right to her left in front of her. She stared in awe at what she sensed God whispering to her.

Darryl and Lluvi's marriage was nothing like their dating years and yet, it still wasn't what Lluvi knew a marriage had the potential to be. Lluvi still found herself battling jealousy which attempted risky invasions and attacks on her marriage. "I am with you my sweet child," she heard God's gentle voice deep in her heart. He continued, "Walking in faith means you can't see it; just as you can't see the wind. But you know the wind is there by what it's producing. You see the evidence. You will see the evidence of your faith.

You will see the results that are coming forth from the unseen. Just as you see the leaves, You will see my power in the midst of this (marriage) journey. You will experience who I am and My unending and unfailing love for you." Lluvi sobbed at this beautiful moment with the Lord.

Her marriage wasn't awful. "Darryl and I have been doing better and better, and yet, why don't I feel like we are? I still feel stuck Daddy," she cried out. "Why do I still feel like hiding and avoiding the hard things?" she continued. "Why do I feel a darkening sensation approaching and carrying all the past hurts to the forefront?" she questioned.

"I am with you, My sweet Lluvi. I am with you." she heard the Lord comfort her. In a more passionate way, she began writing prayers she would need to pray over herself, Darryl, Zaq and Zhandyn. She knew that at some point the filth they had once stored up would soon need to be exposed. She was afraid of what this exposure had the power to do, and yet, she knew God held greater power than whatever was behind that stuffed closet door they stuffed years ago.

Lluvi continually desired for God's presence so she wouldn't face the explosion of the stuffed closet alone with her thoughts. God's Word says that in His presence there is fullness of joy (Psalm 16:11). Throughout their journey toward building solid lives Darryl and Lluvi had been able to fall more and more in love with God. They were in a path that has them experiencing His love, joy, and peace.

Darryl and Lluvi continued to believe that they would be able to see God's power in their marriage. They both understood that God's hand is not shortened. They continued to hold on to God's truth as they rested in the palm of His hand. Lluvi continued to abide in God as she braced for the one day the swinging door of that closet they once sealed would open to destroy their perfectly imagined marriage.

Chapter 13

DECEPTION GAINED POWER

The years together continued full of moments of healing and restoration. A few years after Lluvi's magical moment with God, the wind, and dancing leaves, she understood that somehow the closet was on its verge of explosion. Still, in utter shock and unsure of the cause of the detonation, she faced the eruption without a way of running for cover.

The surprise attack of this missile-like bomb was more than she ever imagined. The thunderous event crashed on top of her in motion to take her out. Had she been in the same space she was 13 years earlier or even 10 years earlier, she would not have been armored and geared for what she was about to discover.

The new year of 2019 started off as all other years did, full of hope and with new set goals. Darryl was traveling for work and loving what he did while Lluvi worked with at-risk youth and loving what she did. Both were in their element and flourishing.

One day after taking home some of her students, Lluvi noticed a small felt bag with marijuana and a pipe in it. Thinking it was one of her students, she turned it in. That same day, Lluvi saw Darryl immensely searching their car. She asked him what he was looking for. "Ahh, I'm looking for my wallet!" he answered. She thought it a little strange to be looking in that area of the car, but she carried on with her homework. She had returned to school to obtain her degree and had little time to focus on more than necessary.

In need of more time with his wife, Darryl planned to take Lluvi with him to one of his business trips to Florida. As they loaded the car for their ride to the airport Lluvi smelt the familiar smell of marijuana as they left the house. Dismissing it and thinking it might have been a skunk, they headed to their little trip.

They enjoyed each other's company as best they could with the workload they both brought with them, but it was their time together that mattered most. They used every opportunity to be together and soak in the warmth of the Florida sun. This was a much needed break from their well known Januaries in Michigan. They had been living in Michigan since fall of 2012 and enjoyed most everything Michigan had to offer but preferred breaks from the long winters.

Darryl and Lluvi returned from their trip and headed back to their normal routines. Zaq was gearing up to graduate and searching for his path to take in life. Zhandyn was enjoying his carefree life as any eight year old does. Life seemed to be all they had ever wished it would be. The American dream was no longer a dream, but their reality. Darryl and Lluvi were no longer enemies nor attacking each other with the sword of their tongues. This life was exactly what they had envisioned and yet something was not kosher.

This inner nagging was taking place in Lluvi's heart. She attempted to resist it and as she did it would become louder and louder. As Darryl prepared to head to work, Lluvi was in search of her hair straightener that she had taken to Florida. She saw his backpack on the living room floor and thought he might have packed it last minute as it might have still been too hot to put in their luggage.

She bent down, unzipped a pocket and almost lost her balance at what she found. A plastic baggie met her eyes. She opened the bag to find a glass pipe, lighter and a small plastic bag with marijuana. Shocked at what she found, her face began to feel hot. The room began to spin. She felt her stomach churn. She heard white noise and started to see white. She regained her balance by the help of the door frame and took in deep breaths. She pieced the incident with Darryl frantically searching the car to this very moment. "The weed was Darryl's!?" She shouted internally. She took the baggie and hid it in her closet.

Lluvi got ready and headed out the door for the staff training she was about to have. The carpooled drive to their destination was full of confusion and tears. Thankfully she weeped by the window of the full van with her hair covering her face. Afraid of being heard and seen, she did her best to refrain from thinking about that morning. She redirected her thoughts constantly, plastered a smile to her face and walked into that training ready for the team-filled activities.

Darryl texted her after shortly arriving at her training. He told her that he found marijuana in the basement and thought it was Zaq's. Lluvi knew deep down inside that this information did not connect the dots that lay before her. She allowed Darryl to continue as his plan was to get to the bottom of it and she didn't have to worry. "Why did Darryl just give me this information?" She wrestled within herself. "What prompted him to share this information now?" She questioned. He was caught and he knew it. He was attempting to slither his way out of this–just like how he would when they were younger

Darryl's instinct when cornered is to wiggle his way out with his words. Lluvi had lived with this man long enough to know what self preservation looked like for him. His form of deception is similar to a magician or an illusionist. They cause the audience to be distracted by having them look in a certain direction while they do something in another direction.

"But Darryl is a new creation!" Lluvi argued silently. This did not make sense to Lluvi at all. She thought they were past the deception and lies. Heat began to fill her whole body and her ears began to ring as she saw the room spin and become bright as the sun. She sat down slowly and took in deep breaths to refill oxygen to her brain.

She collected her thoughts and focused on the training she was a part of. The shock had now turned to sadness at the thought of her husband's deceptions. The years of transparency and vulnerability had given her the practice to allow sadness to live without being morphed into anger. But she feared anger would rise up any moment to protect her.

She mustered up the courage to confront Darryl and asked him directly.

"Is the baggie yours?"

"No." He said in his calm collected voice.

She knew this form of communication far too well.

"Is the *marijuana* yours?"

"No." He again said.

Darryl knew how to answer direct questions. If the marijuana was his friend's he could feel honest about answering the question with a "no." Lluvi knew this about him.

She was short for questions as the confusion of God's truth that Darryl was a new creation and her eye witnessing his transformation made no sense as to why he had weed and lied about it. He redirected her thoughts and lured her to believe it was Zaq's. That was farther away from what she believed the truth to be, but she wanted so badly to believe her husband. She wanted to trust him at his words as she had learned to do throughout their years.

Lluvi approached Zaq and questioned him. Surprised at the question he adamantly denied it to be his. She was experiencing the overwhelming feeling of disorientation once again. She couldn't figure up from down. She threatened to fingerprint the items and to get to the bottom of this.

Fear shook Zaq to his core. What in the world was his mom saying? She would send him to juvi? Does she know what happens there? He knew all too well what that place held for he was on his career path to be in law enforcement. He had toured the county juvenile hall a year prior. After his mom left his room, in panic he reached out to his best friend. He shared his concern and fears. His best friend asked him for the truth. Zaq reassured him it was not his. With a heart for his friend and his predicament, Zaq's friend offered to take the blame if it came down to it. His friend was no stranger to smoking weed.

Lluvi walked into her bedroom perplexed at the situation she was facing. For years their family had been serving in ministry, loving God and loving people. "How did this come about?" She asked herself. Darryl and Lluvi have been on the leadership team at their church and part of the team spearheading the recently launched church campus. This didn't make any sense to her. She didn't know what to do or who to go to.

She reached out to her previous pastor who was part of the new campus launch. He directed her to reach out to the new campus pastors whom she had known for years prior to them becoming her pastors. With the inability to speak for fear she wouldn't hold it together and afraid she'd jumble through her words, she began to draft an email.

She sat shaking on March 9, 2019 to type her thoughts. She was unsure if she would send what she wrote but she knew she had to write it down so her memory would serve her correctly. She was concerned the facts would get manipulated and she'd be forced to question how things played out if she didn't write them out.

> In the beginning of February our transmission went out so I had a rental that week. Darryl had the Prius that whole week. I got it back that Friday and he took his company car home. As I'm getting mine and Zhandyn's backpack out of the Prius something falls out. It's a sunglasses baggie. I thought nothing of it.
>
> I brought everything inside then I noticed a smell coming from that baggie. It's the smell of weed. I open it up and see a pipe and weed and feel a

lighter at the bottom of the baggie. I don't know what to think so I assume it was one of my student's that I took home that day after work. I sent my student a picture of what I found telling him that I think he left this in my car. He asked me what it was and said it wasn't his.

I still assumed it probably belonged to him until Darryl got home. I heard his car pull up but he wasn't coming inside. After a little bit, I go see what's going on and he's searching the Prius. He said he was looking for his wallet.

It looked suspicious to me so I talked with him and told him what I found and asked if he was smoking. I believed him and turned in the baggie to the school's Vice Principal because I thought it was my student's.

Part of me wasn't 100% convinced as for years Darryl tasted and smelled like covered up weed. Every time I brought it up he'd manipulate the conversation and I would end up feeling stupid and crazy for thinking it.

This Friday morning I had a panic attack. We had just gotten back from Florida and I couldn't find my straightener in any of our half unpacked luggages so I looked through his backpack thinking he might have packed it last minute there.

As I'm looking for it I smelt weed. Then I found a sandwich baggie with a pipe, weed, and lighter. My hands started shaking, my heart started going crazy and I had a hard time breathing. I took the baggie and hid it in my closet and tried to get it together.

He got out of the shower and we're getting ready for work. He then starts searching his backpack like crazy. He tells us he's looking for a pack of business cards.

My heart sank when I watched him look through his backpack the way he was searching the car. It was too much of a coincidence and I cried all the way to GR for a workshop.
He texted me later that morning telling me that he found a pipe and weed downstairs that morning and wonders if it's Zaq's or his friend (his friend is the same student I took home the first time I found the bag of weed).

I asked where he found it. He said by our walk out basement door. That doesn't sit right either. He found it? We don't even ever use that door and we're all getting ready for work and he's down there by that door?

Later that day I connected with Zaq about what Darryl said he found. Zaq is adamant that the weed is not his that it can't be his friend's either. I told him that I'll be having him take a urine test and checking fingerprints so the truth better come out before the results do.

He says he's 100% the test will come back clean. He later spoke to his friend who told him it wasn't his but if it was Zaq's that he'll take the blame for it. Zaq told him it wasn't his.

All this points back to Darryl and I can't deny it this time. Last time it was questionable, this time it's too coincidental-like no way! I kept feeling crazy but all of this doesn't add up and I know I'm not going crazy!

I ended up letting Darryl know what I found in his backpack and told him that it doesn't add up and it's too coincidental and he got upset and refuses to take a drug test to give me peace of mind. He wouldn't give a reason, he just came back questioning me for questioning him. He kept saying "like I'm just trying to figure out why you would ask me that and think that I would. What would I gain from smoking?"

No direct answer. It doesn't add up even more. Zaq wants to clear his name and wants to bet me $100 that his test will come back clean and is all for the fingerprinting thing and getting his and his friend's name cleared. Darryl refusing to take the test is causing me to question him even more.

His heart was beating fast too when I brought it up. I could see it through his throat. He said he was a grown man and that if he wanted to smoke it he could. All of this makes my stomach hurt. I haven't been able to build the courage to pull the fingerprints off because I don't want to. I want him to talk to me about this.

This time it just doesn't add up. He "found it" downstairs by the back door? He doesn't go there! We don't use that door for anything! It remains locked and he found it that morning that he happened to be by that door?

Darryl has learned to survive the system by using

> his words. He will time and time again tell me something that is not a lie because I didn't ask the question correctly. This has been the struggle in our relationship for all the years I've known him.
>
> I want to give him the benefit of the doubt but if it was Zaq's friend which doesn't make sense (all my students I have do NOT leave things like this lying anywhere). It's money to them; it's valuable to them to just leave. For him to have left it twice doesn't make sense.
>
> Darryl's behavior, choice words and refusal to take a drug test is very questionable. Could you possibly connect with him? The morning I found it I texted our previous pastor and he encouraged me to let my new pastors know and go to marriage counseling which we plan on it but if this is Darryl's and he is using then being exposed is what he needs in order to walk in freedom.
> He needs someone to partner with him without judgment. I'm really sorry this was so lengthy but I knew I would miss details if we spoke in person. We can still connect tomorrow but at least now you'll have the information beforehand.

Her new pastor said he would connect with Darryl and suggested that Lluvi include his wife in any written correspondences. Unfortunately, the pastor did not end up connecting with Darryl. Lluvi found more questions to ask Darryl. She began to interrogate him and he continued to deny that what she found was his. Lluvi began to feel anger rise up.

She ordered the drug test online and waited to address the situation again.

Before the test came back, she researched the best way to pull fingerprints from objects. She collected the supplies and left the house threatening Darryl that one way or another she would find the truth. She parked in front of her best friend's house and sobbed frantically.

She was a wreck. She walked in and just cried on her couch. She cried the ugly cries of disappointment. Her best friend's husband, who interestingly, happened to be the same Aaron from high school who played football with Darryl, understood her pain.

He had seen her in this pain before. He was also the same friend who shocked Lluvi with his words that she would marry Darryl one day. This same lifelong friend had witnessed their relationship in shambles from Darryl's deceptive ways. Aaron and his wife, Sandra, attempted to comfort Lluvi through her pain, but she just sulked in disenchantment.

The next day, in her quiet time with God, she received a text from Aaron. His gentle yet matter of fact approach to her situation felt familiar. He always seemed like an analyzer at heart; observing intently and only speaking up when needed. His words pierced and penetrated Lluvi's heart. Aaron reminded her of her love for Darryl. He reminded her of Darryl's need to be loved.

"If not you then who? If not now then when?"

were the words that bulged out of her phone. She felt his friendship like one Esther had with Mordacai in the Bible. He was calling her up to see from a new perspective. Not from the place of her pain, but from a much grander location that requires letting go of her limited positional view.

She wiped her tears, repositioned herself and acknowledged her "Esther moment." Walking out a challenge is just that-*challenging!* Lluvi is still human with human characteristics. She knew to love Darryl through this, but didn't know what that looked like for him nor her.

Lluvi was finally able to convince Darryl to take the drug test. He took it and the results caused the reality to sink in deeper than Lluvi knew what to do with. Sobbing uncontrollably she called on Gary & Michelle to help them navigate her through this devastating blow. Michelle could not understand a lot of what Lluvi was attempting to explain, but she understood the heartache. Lluvi sounded devastated and Michelle's concern rose as Lluvi became unable to speak and breath through the horrific wailing.

Gary and Michelle showed up at Darryl and Lluvi's house ready to pour out love to them both. Darryl felt cornered and paced the living room floor as he justified his behavior. "I'm a grown man and can do whatever I want," he exclaimed. Doing whatever he wanted was not the reason Gary and Michelle were there. Smoking weed was not the issue that day. The underlying matter was the lying and deception.

Both Gary and Michelle spoke calmly as if approaching an injured bear with a large spear to its paw. Any sudden movement or fluctuation to their voices could provoke growling and intimidation. By this time, Lluvi was more conscious and no longer under the control of an anxiety attack. She was able to contain her breathing patterns to a healthy pace. She attempted to express her concern for the lying.

Darryl's composure concerned Lluvi. She felt both her pain and his fear. She wanted to sulk in her pain, but was again moved with compassion. Her dear husband who lied was in panic mode and was probably feeling threatened in some way. The scripture in Psalms 17:9 rose to the forefront of her mind. "Whoever covers an offense seeks love…"

Lluvi realized, "Darryl was ashamed of his behavior and the reason he covered up the truth. He was seeking love!" This revelation blasted loudly within Lluvi's painful heartache. The sound of that truth vibrated her heart. The vibration was now rattling, connecting all the broken pieces of her heart back into one.

Chapter 14

GOD RESTORES THE YEARS THE LOCUST HAVE EATEN

Darryl and Lluvi both give and receive love differently. Lluvi, in her limited ways of understanding love through the marriage workshops, reading and applying what she'd learned, found herself stumped at what had gone wrong. Clearly, through the book, The Five Love Languages, she understood how to love Darryl. She would write him letters of affirmation to show she loved him. She would show her support in his endeavors and revealed her admiration to his unwavering endurance level.

Conned once again, Lluvi reverted to believing the lie that she wasn't enough for Darryl. "I am just not enough." She proclaimed. That statement was *not* the lie exactly. The lie was what she was believing through the delivery of this statement. It was bringing forth condemnation. She knew this form of manipulation from her adversary. It was Satan's way of getting her to enter back into her once dark castle of self pity and loneliness.

In that moment, faced with the reality that she was not enough for him, she remembered a moment she had with her Daddy God years prior. Darryl, Zaq and Lluvi were living in a converted bedroom in her parents' house. Zaq was in 2nd grade when Lluvi found herself crying in bed one afternoon. With her Bible soaking up her tears, she heard the tender voice of her Father. She leaned in to listen to His voice. "Man will fail you," she heard. "Darryl will fail you my sweet girl. He is not Me." She digested those words.

While coming back into connection with her present situation, the words "Man will fail me," brought her to a melancholy state, absorbing the truth that she was not enough for Darryl. "Of course! I can't be," she shouted internally. "I too am human with human capacities and limitations. "Yes, I failed him. Of course, I'm not enough for Darryl. I can't possibly be enough for him. Only God can be enough for him!"

This truth penetrated her entire being. She came to a new understanding that Darryl needed a safe place and she was not his safe place. Saddened and alarmed by this truth she weeped at her shortcomings. That crushed her heart even more. She felt Darryl's pain as their eyes met for a glimpse. Darryl was in pain and all she had wanted was answers. She began to forcefully push selfishness out. There was not enough room for both compassion and selfishness to live inside her.

Darryl needs something that she didn't know about, or maybe she did. Multiple times, Darryl attempted to express his feelings only for Lluvi to disregard them because she failed to see that they were feelings. He didn't use "I feel" statements so Lluvi was ignorant to his pain. How could that be possible? They have been married for 13 years now.

Why could she not see what has been happening right in front of her? She felt worse for Darryl. She was still hurt by the lying and deception, but she knew she needed to forgive him. To forgive seemed like a walk in the park compared to trusting him again. That trust would have to be rebuilt. She prayed they would both be up for the challenge.

Although love is what was needed, through this process, Lluvi realized it wasn't being expressed in its truest form; love without boundaries. Love without expectations. Love without judgment is what Darryl needed at that moment. Gary & Michelle continued to love them both and were there to facilitate the raw and real side to marriage in its non-glamorized form.

It was a painful time for all four of them. It pained Gary and Michelle that they could not walk this out for them. Darryl & Lluvi must walk this out together. And they each had to walk things out internally amongst themselves and God. With hugs they said their good-byes. The night ended with Lluvi's head pounding from all the tears she had shed that day.

Darryl and Lluvi began marriage counseling. There, they learned skills to better communicate, but they did not get into the nitty gritty of things. The counselor questioned Lluvi's inability to see a relapse coming. It was something Lluvi should have foreseen because of Darryl's past, she revealed.

Lluvi, in her naive thinking, just couldn't believe it was possible. She had also never used any drugs so she didn't have any experiences to lean on. Although therapy was helping, it was barely scratching the surface. It was gently going through every grain of filth they had shoved in the closet. To sweep up every grain seemed endless. Lluvi wanted the big boulders talked about, then they could work their way to the small things. "Why start with the little things?" She silently questioned. Those all got there because the boulders were scraping against one another causing sand like dust to shed like a Husky sheds in summer.

Darryl was doing his part. He was intentional to show Lluvi he was being honest and speaking truth. He held his tongue when she questioned things. He would hold her, look her in the eyes and embrace every question she had until she felt loved and satisfied with the truth.

Lluvi was cautious in her approach when she

needed answers. She attempted to use her eyes in quest for the truth. Darryl could read her eyes in search of truth. Darryl met her there. They both met each other where they were. Lluvi was in pursuit of truth while Darryl was seeking love and acceptance regardless of his shortcomings. They continued their new level of sensitivity toward each other in hopes they would both be fully accepted by each other.

In moments of disagreements as marriage tends to have (because a perfect marriage does not exist), their boys would lead them together to dance it out. Zaq would lead Lluvi toward Darryl as Zhandyn would lead Darryl toward Lluvi. Disturbed with one another they each reluctantly took one another's hand, but would time and time again choose to dance it off.

The dance floor doesn't lie. Every hesitation or unwillingness to connect is revealed on that dance floor their living room would shift into. Little by little as they danced it off, their hearts would begin to melt for each other once again. Little by little they would feel the power love held. Unknowingly that the dance lessons they took years prior had the capability to bring them toward a place of healing and reconciliation, gratitude filled their hearts for that living room dance floor.

They hadn't realized that October of 2016 would armor them for the moments they would be facing. That 22nd day of October set their marriage toward a different trajectory. They drove away from the restaurant thinking that the free Rumba dance lesson was not going to happen. Strangely, Lluvi turned to face the restaurant on their drive over the Kalamazoo River. She screeched in excitement.

"It's starting now!" she proclaimed. Darryl turned the car around and they partook in the free dance lesson. Throughout the night, they had delightful conversations with the owners of Kalamazoo Ballroom Academy (KBA) and felt an instant connection. The owners shared their heart for marriages which coincidentally (but not really) was the burden on Darryl and Lluvi's heart. They knew where they had been and where they were headed in their walk as husband and wife. They had full expectation for great things to come forth from their new found friends, Brock & Terri at KBA.

Darryl and Lluvi ended up signing up to take their Simply Social beginning group dance lessons. They started taking lessons with the goal of having fun and obtaining a new way to form connections with each other. As they stood listening to Terri's directions, they were in shock to what they heard. Surprised by their instructors' teaching method, they squirmed at the thought of what they said.

Nervously, Lluvi took the hand of the stranger in front of her. He did his part to lead her through the steps instructed to them. In rotation she would dance with the next man in front of her while Darryl danced with other women. This was not the connection she was looking for. It was awkward and she felt disloyal. Although it was explained to them the reason for this style of teaching, it didn't reduce the feelings she was having about Darryl's arm around other women while she faced each man in front of her as they did the same to her.

She tried to understand this method, but argued with the Lord about it. "Daddy, I just don't understand why we need to dance with other people; it doesn't make sense to me." She viewed dancing in a sacred type of way. It felt like a form of expression to her love for Darryl and here she was needing to learn how to dance with strangers.

They continued to take lesson after lesson, week after week without fully understanding why. Then one day on their way to the car from one of the lessons Daddy God's response was tenderly simple. "Dancing is a form of communicating without words," came the revelation. She was beginning to understand every move these men were making to lead her. The simple slightly pressured touch to her back and hand led Lluvi the direction they were leading her. She was understanding why it was easier to follow the lead of some men over others. She pondered on that all the way home.

The following lessons followed the routine patterns of rotating partners. She began to clearly differentiate their non-verbal communication through their gentle yet firm touch. She imagined God being the same way with her. He was not abrasively moving, nor spinning her. If she missed the count or step she was to take, her dance leader would continue the dance to continue to gently lead. She felt guilty for following others' better than Darryl. She tried so hard to follow, but couldn't anticipate his moves all the time. She felt stiff and on edge at times until her dance instructor and new friend, Terri, spoke up.

"Lluvi I can't tell if you're leading or if Darryl is. And if I can't tell if he's leading, then I can't correct him." As Terri's words spoke it was as if the clouds opened up and God Himself said those words to Lluvi. It translated differently into her heart.

"Lluvi my love, you cannot be Darryl's Holy Spirit. When you try, you cause Darryl to focus on you and not Me. I need his attention, but he's giving it to you. Please allow My Spirit to be louder than you." Lluvi was taken back by what she just experienced. She had never seen herself trying to play God and yet, there she stood trying to lead Darryl in their marriage. She was trying to mold him into the image she thought she wanted instead of allowing God's handiwork to craft Darryl into who he was intended to be.

Following Darryl did not come naturally. Lluvi fumbled and would take over every time Darryl missed his steps or derailed off beat. It took more practice than she had anticipated, but over time Lluvi learned this new skill of following her dance partner, her husband. When they faced challenging situations Lluvi would remember that lesson that day. When the song changes they might step on each other's toes, but at the end of the day, it doesn't matter if they miss the beat as long as they stay connected. Again, the dance floor doesn't lie. Are they dancing disconnectedly or with hearts connected? Their love is revealed in how they dance to the songs of life.

On December 1, 2019 Darryl and Lluvi were in service, just like any other Sunday before then. Their pastor spoke words that shook Lluvi to her core. She had heard this being said in her many years of living, but somehow that day, it impacted her to a new degree. "You can't look where you're headed if you keep looking in the rear view mirror" "What areas of my life do I need to let go of?" She wrote in her journal.

Her pastor continued, "God wants to do a new thing. Sometimes we put our sin on a pedestal. You and your sin are not greater than God." That day, that truth began to take root at new depths within her heart. Lying and deceiving are not greater than God in our marriage. Just the same, neither is distrust greater than God, Lluvi concluded. Like Mary in Luke 2:19, Lluvi took these things and pondered them in her heart.

While under a state of emergency, the year 2020 brought forth a new set of challenges around the world. The Covid-19 pandemic brought a mixture of both discomfort and comfort. The weeks of confinement through the quarantine, brought Darryl and Lluvi to an interesting position in their marriage. Lluvi's initial joking reaction was "Oh no! Someone is going to die and someone is going to jail!" Half joking about the state of their marriage, she knew deep down inside this quarantine had the potential to destroy their marriage in the worst possible way.

Living under one roof is one thing. Being confined for long periods of time caused Darryl to get antsy as he would at times experience during long weekends. There was no outlet for him. All business travels had ceased. He loved their home, but to stay home days upon days and weeks upon weeks was no easy task for this social butterfly. Although he did not see himself as an extrovert, as he enjoys his quiet times to refresh, he found no comfort enduring isolation for long periods of time.

Darryl and Lluvi learned many new card games to play in the evenings after their days of video calls while finding their rhythm to working remotely. They no longer had the commute to their employment, so the extra time was now being spent having unrushed family breakfast. Their free moments were spent taking walks around their neighborhood and enjoying the fresh air nature provided. While navigating their new family and individual routines, Lluvi came across an unexpected turn of events.

The past as she had known it was just that–it was left in the past. Both she and Darryl were each doing their part to care for one another's hearts. The way they communicated revealed the levels of growth they both had obtained throughout their years together. To anyone looking in, they would find Darryl and

Lluvi's marriage full of peace and tranquility. Although their former days of shouting fights were a thing of the past. Their marriage was still missing something. Neither could pinpoint what it was and yet the void was known. How to fill it was a mystery. At this point, they were wholeheartedly following God and both loving each other better than years prior.

One day in the midst of the quarantine, Lluvi began searching for something specific in a hand made wooden box that held all her pictures of high school and of Zaqry's younger years. As she searched through the hundreds, possibly thousands of pictures, she stopped. She sat down on the floor. She stared at the inside of the box. In shock of what she was feeling, she hectically grabbed all those pictures. She took them to the basement.

Sorting through their basement full of tools and nick nacks, she found what she needed. She pulled out the heavy bin ready to start fresh without the past haunting her. As she anxiously selected the needed materials, she loaded them onto her arms and raced upstairs to their kitchen. Laying everything on the countertop she began the next steps toward freedom.

One by one each photo was carefully placed into glass frames ready to be displayed on the walls of her home. Up until that moment, her stomach would churn at the sight of seeing their younger selves. Up until that moment, each of those pictures held memories she'd wished she could forget. Up until that moment she was disgusted at the malicious people they once were and the pain she had endured from it. As she continued to see these pictures of themselves at 16 and 17, she felt compassion. She saw these beautiful souls who knew nothing less than being 16 and 17 years of age; unaware of the depth their behavior would cause one another. It truly felt as if her heart had been 10 sizes too small and it was now forming into the size it was designed to be all along.

She saw beauty unfold as she appreciated these teenagers for their tenacity to push through every obstacle that came against them. She cried tears of joy as gratitude embedded every core of the flower filled path that led her away from that once standing castle. This dark castle was no longer occupied. It was vacant. No one lived there anymore. Anger, hate, sadness, resentment and the rest of the once protective emotions were no longer to be found. That castle that was once fortified and indestructible was now but a desolate ruin. Lluvi no longer needed to find it as her fortress. She now lived in the path of flowers away from those ruins.

She took in a peaceful breath as she hung those pictures on her walls. Taking long pauses to breathe in this new found freedom, she knew that she was experiencing the manifestation of God's promise. He truly restores the years the locusts had eaten.

BIBLIOGRAPHY

Alan Guttmacher Institute. (2004). U.S. Teen Pregnancy Statistic: Overall Trends, Trends by Race and Ethnicity And State by State Information. New York: The Alan Guttmacher Institute.

"Allegory of the long spoons." Wikipedia, https://en.wikipedia.org/wiki/Allegory_of_the_long_spoons. Accessed 20 September 2023.

Centers for Disease Control and Prevention. (2019, September 16). Retrieved from Centers for Disease Control and Prevention: https://www.cdc.gov/teenpregnancy/about/index.htm

Dido (2003). White Flag from the album Life for Rent, The Church

Dirmann, D. (2009, September 13). Prayer Life. Lecture presented at Level Four of Operation Solid Lives in The Rock, Anaheim.

Dirmann, J (2007). Operation Solid Lives Intense Discipleship Program, The Rock, Anaheim.

Ligertwood, B. (2023, October 9). Awake My Soul and Sing on Lisa Harper's Back Porch Theology Podcast Retrieved October 15, 2023, from https://www.instagram.com/p/CyT-Y1vuVKz/

Livingwell Pregnancy Centers. (2019, September 16). Retrieved from Livingwell Pregnancy Centers: https://www.living-well.org/learn-about-livingwell

Rogers, A. (2019, August 29). How to Guard Your Heart. Retrieved December 28, 2020, from https://www.biblestudytools.com/bible-study/topical-studies/how-to-guard-your-heart.html

Winkler, K. (2017, October 19). Worship VS Praise - Is There Difference? Retrieved December 27, 2020, from https://www.sharefaith.com/blog/2013/11/worship-praise-difference/

ACKNOWLEDGMENTS

First and foremost, I would like to express my sincere gratitude to my dearest husband & best friend, Darryl, who believed in me and saw the unseen within me. Thank you babe!

I am beyond grateful for my oldest, Zaq, who without his beautiful existence my life would not have unfolded in this magnificent way. You are my sunshine.

I am so grateful for my youngest, Zhandyn, who breathes out love in abundance without restraint. You are my favorite Munk-a-doo.

I would like to highlight two truly exceptional people, my parents, Eduardo & Esmeralda, for pushing through the many obstacles immigrants face so that I could be where I am today.

I want to thank Gary & Michelle Gomez, who loved freely and cared deeply for my marriage and family.

I want to give my deepest appreciation to Beth Bolthouse, my editor, who first suggested publishing my story while reading my Life Learning Essay at Cornerstone University. Beth, thank you for coming alongside me to share this redemptive love story.

I am grateful for my beautiful friend, Sandra De La Cruz, for encouraging me with those powerful words all those years ago, "not everyone has a passion to write, you shouldn't ignore this."

A big thank you to Traci Kelly for being the sounding board I needed in order to finalize all the fine details.

I would also like to extend my gratitude to Nadine Ardnt, who saw my potential at 17 and believed in my ability to write. I wouldn't be here without your support; thank you Nadine.

NOTE FROM THE AUTHOR

I could have chosen another path on that fork all those years ago-but I didn't. Oh how thankful I am that I didn't! Had I avoided the difficulties of parenting and the hardships of the relationship with my son's dad, I would have limited the beauty that came forth from such challenges. How many times do we avoid difficulties throughout our days? More often than we recognize, I'm sure.

Our culture has cultivated us to have such an aversion to pain and hardships. Just look around at all those things at our fingertips and the convenience it brings. We are almost lost without all those comforts. It's unfortunate that we prefer comfort and happiness over people and life. The misalignment of values has the potential to sway us farther away from the beautiful possibilities life can hold. And when we experience the pressures on every side be alert to what gets revealed. That is when what we truly believe gets exposed.

"In 2017, a total of 194,377 babies were born to women aged 15–19 years, for a birth rate of 18.8 per 1,000 women in this age group" (Centers for Disease Control & Prevention, 2019). Although this number is another record low for teens in the United States, it is still a rather large number of babies being born to adolescents—probably due to the convenience abortions bring.

An altering life decision has to be made and I,

along with others, did not want to make it. The teen pregnancy rate in 2000, the year I faced this decision, ranged from 42 (North Dakota) to 128 (Nevada) pregnancies per 1,000 women ages 15-19 (The Alan Guttmacher Institute, 2004). Consequences are part of every decision made; whether good or bad, consequences exist. The options are out there. A life is not like an online order and that can be returned after changing your mind.

If you are on the very fork I found myself in, know the dangers of believing that life can go on as it once through the solution of abortion. It might work for a while, but sooner or later it can haunt you. I have friends who have lived with the grief and regret from their decisions. Thankfully, they have surrendered their secret and are learning to experience freedom from the grief.

Opposition comes in many shapes and sizes. You are the only one that gets to live your life. No one can live it for you. Not your parents, not your friends, not any other person can walk out the consequences to the decision you have made or will make. You are the only one who gets to walk it out.

Choosing life and keeping my baby was one of the best decisions I have ever made. My son is a young man now and living the life that belonged to him. This aversion to pain or being uncomfortable has the great potential to hinder our life greatly. An athlete understands the pain it must endure to achieve his/her goal. Why is life, as a whole, any different?

I have spoken to women who unfortunately did not have the same support I did and chose to have an abortion. It's sad to see regret and shame have the best of them. Our culture has a way of exalting instant gratification without realizing the blindspots to see what's on the horizon. This instant solution comes with a price–it can come with a lifetime supply of regrets.

Facing this fork on the road was a learning experience that has helped me to see the many invisible forks that I walk through daily. These forks hold many more learning moments within them. Life is full of learning moments; I just need to take the time to see the "beauty in the process."

My hope for you, if you are finding yourself in a similar situation, is that you too would find hope. My life now feels like a fairy tale. Although life is not perfect and there are still its ups and downs, I would never have imagined my life to have transpired the way it did. I am in awe at what God can do with such a toxic and broken heart once fully surrendered. There is nothing too great for God! Oh how I had made Him in my image.

If you are facing an unplanned pregnancy right now, from my heart to yours, I want you to know that you are not alone. The resources are endless. If you are facing the very fork I was facing, I encourage you to visit: https://helpinyourarea.com/ to find a Crisis Pregnancy Center near you. They will listen to your concerns, educate you on the options, and come alongside you in this journey.

If you are living with the consequences or ramifications of an abortion, my heart goes out to you. I want you to know that you too are not alone. I encourage you to visit https://helpinyourarea.com/ or join/start a group using the books. These resources have brought healing to many who have experienced the guilt of abortion.

Surrendering the Secret: Healing the Heartbreak of Abortion by Patricia Layton

A Choice to Remember: The First Step to Your Post-Abortion Healing Journey by Polly Lunetto

If you find yourself a parent, lover, teacher, coach, neighbor, friend, relative, etc. to a pregnant teenager, don't lose heart. Continue to be there in support through the roller coaster that it may bring. They are worth it! And not only for the mom, but the dads need your love and care as well. Oh how thankful I am for those that came alongside my son's dad during his most years.

I implore you, don't give up on them. They need you more than they know how to express. 1 Corinthians 13:13 reminds us that these three remain, faith, hope, and love, but the greatest of these is love. *Be* love to those around you. I'm rooting for you as you come alongside these sweet and precious souls.

ABOUT THE AUTHOR

Lluvia Jeanette Diaz-Lanier was born in Fullerton, California where she spent her childhood & young adult life. She is a first generation Mexican-American daughter born to loving Mexican parents. In her late 20's she, her husband & two sons moved to Southwest Michigan. In 2022, she & her family moved across the country again & now reside in beautiful Southwest Washington where she continues to love God and love people.

She is a proud co-owner of Beloved, a scripture jewelry & apparel company, that Gary & Michelle founded & have franchised. She gets to minister to people all throughout her day just by testifying of the more abundant life that she gets to experience with Jesus.

She & her husband run Dynamic Solutions where they support local businesses & organizations through biblical leadership coaching, training, & more. She is passionate about helping people silence all other voices so they can hear the voice of God and His leading for themselves.

She & her family enjoy the beauty of life together with lots of game nights full of food, fun, & laughter. She loves woodworking & building projects far too big for her skill set, along with sewing & refashioning her clothes to fit her unique style. Above all her doing, Lluvi enjoys just *being* barefoot in the midst of sunshine.

Turn the page for a preview of Lluvia DíazLanier's upcoming book

Growing Up Together

A Teenage Mother's Journey

Chapter 1

THE FORK

There are moments in life we recognize to be forks on the road. Those moments where we take time to consider all factors involved. Those moments that define who we are and that test our character. Those moments that will forever change the course of our lives. But then there are moments where we fail to see those exact forks. We have somehow become blinded by distractions. Blinded the same way a mirror reflects the sun and shines so brightly in one direction, hiding the very thing in front of us. And without recognizing it, we end up deciding on a path without ever seeing, nor considering the remaining paths that laid before us.

In such a moment I had found myself. Puzzled by the fork I had in front of me, I sat there speechless. Not quite understanding how I even got there. I stood still, lacking the knowledge of when I had even stepped foot on that road. I had walked there myself. I knew that much, as no one can walk this life in my place. I sat there perplexed by a forked path I never saw coming several steps prior.

After the shock of this unforeseen fork wore off,

I faced a much bigger, much larger challenge. Fear. Fear began to creep in and remind me of my past mistakes. I was reminded of all my failures. The list was extensive and yet it raced through my mind at such high speed. This very decision would shake the very core of my foundation. Everything I knew to be who I was, was being challenged. Everything was at stake. Everything would change. But little did I know what *everything* truly entailed.

We only get to see the outcome of the decisions made. We never see the outcome of the decisions we passed by. But our mind has a way of making us see the unseen; to see what could have been. And if those thoughts are let loose and uncontrolled, we come face to face with regret. Regret has an interesting way of eating away at our joy. It slowly nibbles and consumes our happiness. If allowed, it even has the power to derail us and throw us off our feet into a pit of darkness where depression awaits.

I knew that day that I didn't want to face regret. I had to make the decision to decide to never go back on that forked road; never to wonder what could have been. But instead, only to embrace the many forks that await this challenging journey I was about to walk in. I could foresee this path costing me more than what I had. I was young and alone. I lacked preparation, diligence, and endurance. I did not have a plan. Benjamin Franklin said, "if you fail to plan, you are planning to fail", and yet my plan was never to fail. In that moment, though, in the midst of fear, I already felt like a failure.

As I set my heart to move in the direction I knew to be the path I wanted to take, I saw the many sacrifices I would face. "Was I strong enough to endure this journey?", seemed to be the question on the forefront of my mind. As my feet began walking out the path I had decided to take, I reminded myself that I myself made this decision. No one chose it for me. I was not forced nor coerced into this decision. I alone get to decide which path to take.

"I chose you. I love you my sweet boy. Choosing you is the best decision I have ever made." are the words inscribed on my son's heart. Growing up together was not easy for the both of us and yet, it was the very aspect that led us to remain as close as we are. As a young man, my son does not resist the love and comfort I can bring as he faces the adversities of life.

As we listen to the sound of the rain outside, I stroke his hair with my hands while his head lies on a pillow by my lap. We can rest in each other's sweet presence without saying a word and understanding the pain that heartbreaks bring. Knowing that this pain does not last forever is what brings forth the peace we need to take a new step each day to come. This pain as intense as it can be does not have the power to define us. "Weeping may endure for a night, but joy comes in the morning."(Psalm 30:5)

Made in the USA
Coppell, TX
24 June 2026

82892840R10125